f ly to another world when you read. Word by word, these stories take you away– to Africa, to China, to the bottom of the sea, and back to the house next door. Just follow the words. Like golden threads they will weave the most amazing sights. A rainbow-colored horse? Imagine that! You'll find it in...

GOLDEN THREADS

Senior Author
John J. Pikulski

Senior Coordinating Author
J. David Cooper

Senior Consulting Author
William K. Durr

Coordinating Authors
Kathryn H. Au
M. Jean Greenlaw
Marjorie Y. Lipson
Susan Page
Sheila W. Valencia
Karen K. Wixson

Authors
Rosalinda B. Barrera
Ruth P. Bunyan
Jacqueline L. Chaparro
Jacqueline C. Comas
Alan N. Crawford
Robert L. Hillerich
Timothy G. Johnson
Jana M. Mason
Pamela A. Mason
William E. Nagy
Joseph S. Renzulli
Alfredo Schifini

Senior Advisor
Richard C. Anderson

Advisors
Christopher J. Baker
Charles Peters

HOUGHTON MIFFLIN COMPANY   BOSTON
Atlanta   Dallas   Geneva, Illinois   Palo Alto   Princeton   Toronto

Beverly Cleary

BOOK 1

THEME BOOK
Ramona Quimby, Age 8
by Beverly Cleary

MYSTERIES OF THE DEEP

BOOK 2

THEME BOOK
Sunken Treasure
by Gail Gibbons

Once Upon A Time

BOOK 3

THEME BOOK
Beauty and the Beast *by Jan Brett*

GLOSSARY
200

AUTHOR

Illustrations by Renée Williams

Beverly Cleary

Dear Houghton Mifflin Boys and Girls,

When I was in the third grade, I suddenly discovered that reading was interesting, exciting, and fun. Books were no longer just something children had to work at in school. From that time on, I went to school to learn what adults felt I needed to know; I went to the library to find what I wanted to learn.

What I wanted to learn was the use of my imagination. Every few days, on trips to our branch library, I checked out fairy tales, myths, legends, mysteries, Heidi, Pinocchio, all the stories I could understand and some I couldn't. The library was my best friend.

However, as I read my way through the library shelves, I discovered something was missing: stories about ordinary American children who lived in the sort of neighborhood I lived in and went to a school like mine, children who played together and whose parents sometimes did not have enough money but managed somehow.

10

Because I loved reading so much, I naturally wanted to create stories of my own. Years passed. One day I said to myself in a stern voice, "If you are ever going to write, do it."

I sat down at an old kitchen table and wrote *Henry Huggins*, which, to my surprise, was accepted by the first publisher I sent it to. Henry was followed by Ellen, Otis, Ramona, Beezus, Ribsy, and my other characters, ordinary Americans, all of them — except for Ralph, the motorcycle-riding mouse.

Since the third grade, books have been an important part of my life. The library is still my best friend. By now I hope you have discovered what friends books can be and that they will be friends all your lives.

Beverly Cleary

Welcome to the neighborhood. This is where many of Beverly Cleary's famous characters live. Henry Huggins and his dog live here, and Ramona and Beezus, too. You will even find Otis Spofford somewhere nearby.

This neighborhood may look like yours, or it may look very different. But in your neighborhood there are sure to be children like Henry, Ramona, and Otis. There may even be a dog that reminds you of Ribsy.

CONTENTS

From the book
Henry and the Clubhouse

Henry Writes

Henry Huggins is the youngest paper boy in his neighborhood. He is trying very hard to show that he is serious about this job, but his biggest problem is five-year-old Ramona Quimby. Ramona follows Henry along on his route, causing one problem after another. The only thing Ramona enjoys more than pestering Henry is the Sheriff Bud television program.

Henry has decided that if he is going to keep his paper route, he will have to do something about Ramona.

a Letter

"SAY, MOM," Henry said one evening, "how can I keep Ramona from being such an awful pest all the time?"

"Just don't pay any attention to her," answered Mrs. Huggins.

"But Mom," protested Henry. "You don't know Ramona."

Mrs. Huggins laughed. "Yes, I do. She is just a lively little girl who gets into mischief sometimes. Ignore her, and she will stop bothering you. She only wants attention."

Henry could not help feeling that his mother did not understand the situation. He had ignored Ramona. That was the whole trouble. He was not paying any attention to her so he had found himself locked in the clubhouse. This was not a little mischief. It was a terrible thing for her to do.

"Surely you are smarter than a five-year-old," remarked Mr. Huggins jokingly.

Henry did not have an answer for his father, who, after all, was safe in his office all day and did not know what a nuisance Ramona could be.

Next Henry consulted Beezus. "Ramona sure causes me a lot of trouble on my route," he remarked one afternoon. "Isn't there some way to get her to stop pestering me?"

Beezus sighed. "I know. I've told Mother, and Mother has told her to behave herself, but you know how Ramona is. She never listens."

"I know," Henry said gloomily. Ramona was a real problem. When Mrs. Quimby persuaded her to stop doing one annoying thing, Ramona promptly thought up something entirely new but equally annoying. If only Henry could find a way to stay ahead of Ramona. . . .

One afternoon Henry arrived at Mr. Capper's garage in plenty of time to fold his papers. He counted his stack of forty-three *Journals* and as long as he was early, he took time to glance through the paper. He looked at the headlines and read the comic section. Then a picture of a smiling lady caught his eye. It was the lady who gave people advice when they wrote to her about their problems.

Because he had a problem, Henry paused to
read her column. A girl who signed her letter
"Flat Broke" said that her father did not give
her a big enough allowance. Her father did not
understand that she needed more money for
school lunches, bus fare, and other things.
What should she do about it? The smiling lady
told her to talk it over with her father and
explain to him exactly what her expenses were.
The smiling lady was sure he would understand.

Henry thought this over. Maybe he should
write to the lady about Ramona. He could
write, I have a problem. A girl in my
neighborhood has a little sister who pesters me
on my paper route. How can I get her to stop?
Then he could sign the letter Disgusted.

Henry tried to think how the lady would answer his letter. Dear Disgusted, she would say, but what would she say next? Probably she would tell him to talk his problem over with Ramona's mother and everything would be all right. Oh no, it wouldn't, thought Henry, just as if he had really read an answer to a letter he had really written. Ramona's mother knew all about his problem and had not been able to solve it. As Beezus said, Ramona never listened very much.

Henry began to fold his papers. There must be somebody Ramona would listen to. And then a picture in an advertisement gave Henry an idea. Santa Claus! Ramona might listen to Santa Claus. Henry grinned to himself. He would really fix Ramona if he waited until Christmas Eve and climbed up on the Quimbys' roof and yelled down the chimney in a deep bass voice, Ho-ho-ho, Ramona Geraldine Quimby, you stop pestering Henry Huggins on his paper route or I won't leave you any presents. Ho-ho-ho.

"Ho-ho-ho," said Henry out loud, to see how much like Santa Claus he could sound.

Just then Mr. Capper came out of the back door. "Who do you think you are? Santa Claus?" he asked.

"No, sir." Embarrassed, Henry went on folding papers.

Still, Henry was pleased with this picture of
himself ho-ho-hoing down the chimney at
Ramona, but unfortunately there was just one
thing wrong with it. Boys were not allowed to
go climbing around on their neighbors' roofs on
Christmas Eve or any other time. And anyway,
Ramona might not even listen to Santa Claus.
Henry would not be at all surprised.

Henry was zigzagging down the street on
his bicycle, throwing papers to the right and to
the left, when he saw Beezus and Ramona
hurrying along the sidewalk. Ramona was
wearing a mustache cut from brown paper and
stuck to her upper lip with Scotch tape. Henry

recognized this as another attempt to copy one of Sheriff Bud's disguises.

"Hi, Beezus," he said.

Ramona pulled at Beezus' hand. "Come on," she said. "Come on, or we'll be late."

"I can't understand it," remarked Beezus. "She can't even tell time, but she always knows when it's time for the Sheriff Bud program."

"Like Ribsy," said Henry. "He can't tell time either, but he always knows when it's time to meet me after school." He pedaled on down the street, when suddenly a thought struck him. *Sheriff Bud.* If there was anyone Ramona would listen to, it was Sheriff Bud.

Henry was so excited by this inspiration that he threw a paper on the wrong porch and had to go back to get it. Of course she would listen to Sheriff Bud, but how could Henry get

Sheriff Bud to tell Ramona to stop pestering him on his paper route? Write him a letter, that's what he would do. Sheriff Bud was always waving around handfuls of letters and wishing listeners happy birthdays and hoping they would get over the measles or something. He was always pretending he could see people in the television audience, too. Henry had never heard him tell a listener to stop pestering someone, but there was no reason why he couldn't. It would be worth trying anyway.

As soon as Henry finished his route he went home and turned on the television set. There was Sheriff Bud in his ten-gallon hat. This time he was wearing a false nose. He held a microphone in one hand, and between commercials was interviewing a row of children who had microphones hung around their necks. All the children said hello to many, many friends out in television land. Henry thought it was a silly program, although he still sometimes watched the cartoons that were shown between the endless commercials.

Ordinarily when Henry wrote a letter he used the typewriter, because it was more fun than pen and ink, but today he was in too much of a hurry to hunt around and poke all those keys. He found a piece of paper and a pen, and after his address and the date, began, "Dear Sherrif." That looked peculiar so he added another *f*. "Dear Sherriff" still looked peculiar so he consulted the dictionary.

Then Henry tore up his letter and started over. "Dear Sheriff Bud," he wrote in his best handwriting. "I need your help. There is this girl who pesters me on my paper route. She always watches your program so could you please tell her to stop pestering me? Her

name is Ramona Geraldine Quimby. Thank you." Then he signed his name, addressed an envelope to Sheriff Bud in care of the television station, found a stamp, and went out to mail the letter.

As soon as the mailbox clanked shut, Henry knew his scheme would not work. Sheriff Bud received thousands of letters every week. He was always talking about the thousands of letters he received. He waved great handfuls of them around. Why would he pay any attention to one letter and a pretty smudgy one, at that?

But doubtful as he was, Henry somehow hung on to a faint hope that Sheriff Bud might really read his letter and help him out. The letter would be delivered the next day but he might not have time to read it before the program went on the air. Maybe the day after . . .

Two days later Henry rang the Quimbys' doorbell about the time the Sheriff Bud program was starting. "Hello, Beezus," he said, when his friend opened the door. "I was wondering — how about a game of checkers before I start my route?"

Beezus looked surprised. She and Henry used to play checkers often, but since he had become a paper carrier and spent so much time working on the clubhouse, he had not found time to play with her. "Why . . . yes, come on in."

As Henry had expected, Ramona was sitting on a hassock in the living room watching Sheriff Bud, who today was wearing sideburns. While Beezus got out the checker set, Henry watched the program.

"And I want all you little folks out in T.V. land to do something for old Sheriff Bud," the Sheriff was saying. "I want you to tell Mother right now, *right this very minute,* to put Crispy Potato Chips, the potato chips positively guaranteed never to bend, on her shopping list. Yes, sirree, this *very minute.*" His smile filled the whole screen.

"Mother!" called Ramona. "Sheriff Bud says —"

"I don't care what Sheriff Bud says," answered Mrs. Quimby from the kitchen. She sounded very cross. "I can make out my grocery list without that man's help."

Beezus set up the checker board on the coffee table and, kneeling, she and Henry began to play. For once Ramona did not bother them, but Henry found it difficult to think about the game and try to follow Sheriff Bud at the same time. They both stopped playing whenever a cartoon came on, but Beezus had no trouble beating him twice in succession.

Once when the sheriff waved a sheaf of letters Henry's hopes rose, but Sheriff Bud only wished a lot of people happy birthday and told how many people had written in to say they liked Nutsies, the candy bar chockfull of energy. Henry wished he had said in his letter that both he and Ramona ate Nutsies all the time. And Crispy Potato Chips, too.

By the time the program had ended Beezus had defeated Henry a third time. Naturally Henry could not let this record stand. "I bet I can beat you tomorrow," he volunteered.

"I bet you can't," said Beezus, "but you can come over and try."

Henry left, and by working fast delivered all his papers on time. The next afternoon he once more presented himself at the Quimbys' front door, this time to show Beezus he really could beat her at checkers. He would forget all about Sheriff Bud. It had been silly of him to think his letter would be read out of all the thousands the television station received. Beezus had the checkers waiting on the coffee table and as usual Ramona was sitting on the hassock watching Sheriff Bud, who was wearing a pair of large false ears. His voice filled the living room.

"Ramona, turn that program down!" called Mrs. Quimby from the kitchen.

Ramona did not budge.

This time Henry was determined to ignore even the cartoons. Beezus made the first move with a red checker and Henry moved his black checker. Beezus jumped him, he jumped her, and the game was on.

"And now, kiddies out there in T.V. land, if Mother doesn't have a cupboard full of —" Sheriff Bud was saying.

Mrs. Quimby appeared in the living room. "Ramona, turn that thing off. I am sick and tired of listening to that man tell me what to buy."

"No!" screamed Ramona. "No! I don't want to turn it off."

"Then turn it *down,*" said Mrs. Quimby, and went back into the kitchen. This time Ramona lowered the sound of the television set slightly.

"Your move," Beezus reminded Henry.

Henry studied the board. If he moved there, Beezus could jump him. If he moved there, he could jump her if she moved her man in the right direction.

"And now for today's mail," announced Sheriff Bud.

Henry could not help glancing at the television screen. Sheriff Bud was holding the usual handful of letters, but this time he was pointing straight ahead at someone in the television audience. "Ramona Geraldine Quimby, I see you out there," he said. "I see you out in T.V. land."

Henry and Beezus dropped their checkers. Mrs. Quimby stepped out of the kitchen. Ramona clasped her hands together and her eyes grew round. "He sees me," she said in awe.

"Ramona Geraldine Quimby," said Sheriff Bud, "I want you to do something that will make old Sheriff Bud very, very happy."

"Whatever it is, I'm not going to buy it." Mrs. Quimby sounded indignant.

Ramona leaned forward, her eyes wide, her mouth open.

Henry's eyes were just about as wide and his mouth was open, too.

Sheriff Bud sounded as if he and Ramona were alone. "Ramona, it will make old Sheriff Bud very, very happy if you stop

pestering" — he stopped and squinted at a letter in his hand — "Henry Huggins on his paper route. Do you promise?"

"Yes." Ramona barely whispered.

"Good," said Sheriff Bud. "We've got to get those papers delivered. If you stop pestering Henry on his route, you will make me just about as happy as it would if you told Mother you wanted Crispy Potato Chips for lunch every day. And now —"

But no one was listening to the television set.

"Henry!" shrieked Beezus. "Did you hear that?"

"I sure did." Henry was feeling a little awed himself. It had seemed as if Sheriff Bud really could see Ramona. He could not, of course, but . . .

"Honestly!" Mrs. Quimby snapped off the television set. "That man will do anything to squeeze in more commercials. Crispy Potato Chips! Really!"

Only Ramona was silent. She did not even object to her mother's turning off the television set. She turned to Henry with her eyes wide with awe. "Do you really know Sheriff Bud?" she asked.

"Well . . . I guess you might say he is a friend of mine," said Henry and added, to himself, Now.

Then Mrs. Quimby spoke to her youngest daughter. "Ramona, have you been pestering Henry on his paper route again?"

Ramona looked as if she were about to cry. "I — I won't do it any more," she said.

"That's a good girl," said Mrs. Quimby. "Delivering papers is an important job and you mustn't get in Henry's way."

"I bet I know how Sheriff Bud knew about it," said Beezus with a smile. "Your move, Henry."

Henry grinned as he advanced his checker. Beezus promptly jumped and captured two of his men. Oh, well, what did he care? It was only a game. His paper route was real.

Henry grimaced at Ramona who smiled back almost shyly. Henry moved another checker, which Beezus captured. He did not care. His paper route was safe from Ramona. If she pestered him again, all he had to do was to say, "Remember Sheriff Bud," and his troubles would be over. It was as easy as that. He had finally hit upon a good idea that had nothing wrong with it. Not one single thing.

"I won!" Beezus was triumphant.

"I'll beat you in the next game," said Henry, and this time he was sure he would.

Henry thinks his problems are over, but they are really just beginning. You can read what happens next in the book *Henry and the Clubhouse*.

Tell 'em, Sheriff Bud

If you could have Sheriff Bud give a message to one of your friends, what would you ask him to say? Write a letter to Sheriff Bud about your friend. Be sure you explain who your friend is, what your message should say, and why you want Sheriff Bud to give that message to your friend.

OTIS'S
SCIENTIFIC
EXPERIMENT

ONE MONDAY MORNING when Otis went into Room Eleven, he saw an excited group of boys and girls crowded around the ledge under the windows. I wonder what they're looking at, he thought, and climbed up on a desk so he could see over their heads.

He saw two small wire cages. In each cage was a white mouse. Well! Mice in the schoolroom, thought Otis. They should be good for some excitement. Otis liked animals, but Mrs. Brewster, the manager of the apartment house where he lived, did not allow dogs or cats. Until now he had not thought of a pet mouse.

Mrs. Gitler came into the room. "Otis, you know good citizens don't stand on desks," she said, and Otis jumped down.

The whole class began to ask questions. "What are the mice doing here?" "Do we get to keep them?"

Mrs. Gitler smiled. "Take your seats, boys and girls, and I'll explain. They are not white mice. They are baby white rats. Our room is going to perform a scientific experiment."

The class was impressed. "Scientific experiment" sounded important, especially if it meant they could have rats in the schoolroom. And baby rats were much more interesting than grown-up white mice.

Mrs. Gitler went on. "This week we are going to talk about good food. These two

33

baby rats are exactly the same weight. Each weighs forty grams. We are going to feed one of them the same food we eat for lunch in the cafeteria. The other we will feed white bread and soda pop. We will weigh them once a week for three weeks to see which one grows faster."

The class liked this plan. Otis thought it would be fun, too, even though he knew how the experiment would turn out. Mrs. Gitler would never do anything to prove that the baby rats should drink soda pop. She would be on the side of milk and vegetables and that whole-wheat bread they always had in the cafeteria.

Ellen raised her hand. "May we name the rats?"

"That is an excellent idea," said Mrs. Gitler.

"Are they boy rats or girl rats?" someone wanted to know.

"Boy rats," said Mrs. Gitler. "They are twin brothers."

Stewy raised his hand. "We could name one rat Otis."

Everyone laughed loudly at this except Otis, who made a face at Stewy.

Then Patsy suggested Pinky, because the rats had pink ears and tails. Although some of the boys objected, the girls all agreed that Pinky was a good name.

Otis, who thought Pinky was a sissy name for a boy rat, waved his hand. "I think Mutt is a good name for the rat that gets the soda pop."

"Me, too," said George, and the others agreed.

Mrs. Gitler smiled. "It looks as if the soda-pop rat is named Mutt."

Otis looked at Mutt and almost felt as if the little rat belonged to him, because he had named him. He watched Mutt sniff around his cage. Sometimes Mutt stopped to scratch himself with his front paw. Once he scratched with his hind paw like a dog. After a while he settled into a corner of his cage. He put his head down, wrapped his hairless pink tail around his body, and went to sleep.

All morning Otis thought about the rats and wondered how he could use them to stir up some excitement. After lunch the class gathered around the ledge to watch the rat monitors lift the wire cages and set down dishes of food from the cafeteria for the two little animals. Pinky was served tiny bits of macaroni and cheese, green beans, carrot and raisin salad, whole-wheat bread, and raspberry jello. Pinky also had a few spoonfuls of milk. Mutt had a whole saucer of soda pop and half a slice of white bread. Poor Mutt, thought Otis, as he watched the

little rat lap up the pop. Bread and soda pop did not look like much lunch, even for a rat.

After school Otis lingered by the rats' cages instead of trying to be the first one out of the classroom. He had several ideas for stirring up excitement, but there was something wrong with every one of them. Let the rats out of their cages? No. Mutt might get lost or stepped on. Switch cages? Too easy for Mrs. Gitler to guess. Hide one of the rats in Mrs. Gitler's desk? She was not the kind of teacher to scream at the sight of a rat. Hide a rat in Ellen's raincoat pocket? Well, that might do if he couldn't think of anything better. It was the sort of thing any boy might think of. Otis wanted to do something unusual.

By Thursday the children could see that Pinky was already larger than Mutt. His eyes were bright and his fur was glossy. Mutt spent most of his time in the corner of his cage, looking cross. The class could hardly wait until Monday, when Mrs. Gitler would weigh the rats.

When Monday came she took Pinky out of his cage and set him on the scale. He weighed ninety grams, more than twice what he had weighed a week before. Mutt weighed forty-six grams. He had gained scarcely at all. Room Eleven was proud when Miss Joyce brought her class in to see the scientific experiment.

A whole week had gone by. I can't waste any more time, Otis said to himself. Now I've got to think of something. And that day he did.

At noon, when Otis took his place in the hot-food line in the cafeteria, he noticed everyone making faces. When he looked at the steam table to see what they were having for lunch, Otis not only made a face, he groaned and held his nose. They were having scalloped potatoes with some kind of meat, Swiss chard, sliced beets, and rice pudding. And, of course, milk and whole-wheat bread.

"Of all the awful lunches," complained George, who was standing behind Otis.

"It sure is," agreed Otis. "I don't see why we can't have hot dogs and ice cream every day." He gloomily handed the cashier his money. Twenty perfectly good cents wasted, he thought, as he carried his tray to a table. Scalloped potatoes and Swiss chard! Otis carefully picked the meat out of his potatoes and ate that first.

"I'm sure glad I brought my lunch," said Tommy, who was sitting across from Otis, eating the centers out of his sandwiches.

"You're lucky," agreed Otis, poking at his Swiss chard. "I don't see why this stuff would even be good for a rat."

Hey, wait a minute, Otis suddenly thought. He was about to have an idea. He could feel it coming on. This might be very

good food for a rat. If he gave Mutt good food, without anybody's seeing him, Mutt might outgrow Pinky. That would really fix the experiment, because everybody would think it was white bread and soda pop that had made Mutt grow. He could just see Mrs. Gitler's face. And boy, oh, boy, the cafeteria would have to start serving soda pop! That was the best part of all. Soda pop in the cafeteria!

Otis was so pleased with his inspiration that he ate his beets and Swiss chard without even thinking about them. It was a perfect idea. Difficult, of course, but worth it. Already he could see cases of orange and pink and green soda pop stacked in the cafeteria. Now all he had to do was figure out what to feed Mutt and how to slip the food to him without being seen.

That evening Otis went into the kitchen, where his mother was preparing dinner. She was in a hurry, because she had got home late from the Spofford School of the Dance. Otis watched her drop a slab of frozen peas into boiling water and put two frozen cubed steaks into a frying pan. "I'm hungry," he said. "We had an awful lunch at school today."

The peas boiled over onto the stove. "Run along, dear, and don't bother me," said Mrs. Spofford, wiping up the stove. "Mother has been teaching tap dancing all afternoon and she's tired."

Otis leaned against the refrigerator. "Say, Mom, isn't there something that's better for people to eat than scalloped potatoes?"

Mrs. Spofford forked two potatoes baking in the oven. "Why, almost anything, I suppose. Milk and cheese and — oh, I don't know. Lots of things."

Cheese! Of course! Rats liked cheese. He should have thought of that himself. Otis helped himself to a piece of cheese from the refrigerator. Then he noticed a bottle of vitamin pills on the drain board. "Say, Mom, can I have some vitamins?" he asked.

"Yes, dear. Now please run along," said Mrs. Spofford, as she turned the flame down under the meat.

Otis added a handful of vitamin pills to the piece of cheese in his pocket. Cheese and vitamins. They ought to make Mutt grow. Now all he had to do was to find a way to slip them into Mutt's cage without being seen. That was the hardest part of his plan.

When Otis arrived at school early the next morning, he found the door of Room Eleven locked. In a few minutes Mrs. Gitler appeared with the key in her hand. "Good morning, Otis," she said. "My, aren't you bright and early?"

"I . . . uh . . . thought I'd come early and study my spelling," Otis explained. If only Mrs. Gitler would unlock the door and go away.

"Splendid," said Mrs. Gitler, giving Otis a surprised look. Or was it a suspicious look? Otis couldn't tell.

When Mrs. Gitler was busy writing some arithmetic problems on the blackboard, Otis left his desk and went to the rats' cages. Mutt was huddled miserably in a corner. Otis put his hand in his pocket and broke off a piece of cheese.

"Otis," said Mrs. Gitler, without even turning around to look at him, "if you aren't going to study your spelling, you must go out on the playground until the bell rings."

Otis took his seat. He had said he had come early to study spelling, so he supposed he had to sit there with a book in front of him.

All morning Otis waited for a chance to slip food into Mutt's cage. By lunch period he was forced to form another plan. He went into the cloakroom and pretended he could not find his sweater. Then he waited quietly until all the other boys and girls left the room. He heard Mrs. Gitler shut the door. Then he heard something he did not expect. The key turned in the lock. Otis was locked in.

As long as the door was locked, he did not have to worry about being discovered. That was something. Stooping, so he could not be seen through the windows, Otis hurried to the rats. When he lifted Mutt's cage and put down a piece of cheese and a vitamin pill, the little rat scurried over to the food and nibbled greedily.

Good old Mutt. He must have been awfully hungry. The trouble was, Mutt wasn't the only one who was hungry. Otis was hungry too. He wondered what the others were eating in the cafeteria. Maybe it was hot-dog day. Otis watched Mutt finish the cheese and gnaw the vitamin pill, which slipped away from him until he learned to hold it with his paws. Otis was so hungry that he took the rest of the cheese out of his pocket. It was covered with fuzz, but he didn't care. He gave Mutt another piece and ate the rest himself. When it was time for the bell to ring again, Otis made sure there were no telltale crumbs in the cage before he hid in the cloakroom once more.

"Where were you?" Stewy asked, when Mrs. Gitler unlocked the door and the class streamed into the room. "I didn't see you in the cafeteria."

"Oh, around," said Otis vaguely, as he joined the group watching the monitors feed the rats. So it really had been hot-dog day in the cafeteria! Watching Pinky nibble a piece of hot dog made Otis hungrier than ever.

"Mutt isn't eating his bread," someone said. "Do you suppose he's sick?"

"He's probably just tired of it," said Ellen. "You'd get tired of it too, if that's all you had to eat." Then she added, "Poor little Mutt."

The next day Otis brought more cheese and another vitamin pill to Mutt. He also brought a sandwich and a cupcake for himself, so he and the rat ate lunch together. Otis thought Mutt had grown a little already. If only he could keep on feeding him without being caught!

The third day, Otis decided not to feed the rat at noon. Stewy had asked too many questions about why he wasn't in the cafeteria.

"I think Mutt's growing," Otis heard someone say.

"So do I. His stomach sticks out," Tommy said. "And he's frisky, too. Look at him."

Otis was delighted with the way his private experiment was turning out. Just wait till Mrs. Gitler weighed Mutt. When he asked her if she didn't think the cafeteria should serve soda pop, she wouldn't have a thing to say against it.

As he was leaving the room for recess, Otis made a detour past the cages in the hope that he could slip Mutt's food to him.

Stewy followed close at his heels. "What are you tagging around after me for?" Otis asked.

"I'm just looking at the rats," said Stewy. "What would I tag after you for?"

Otis decided he had better be quiet. He did not want to make Stewy suspicious.

When Otis had no better luck feeding Mutt at lunch time, he began to be uneasy. What if he couldn't get any food to Mutt? Maybe the rat would lose weight and he would have to start his experiment all over again.

Finally, as the class left the room to go to the auditorium for folk dancing, Otis managed to slip Mutt's food into the cage. Then he worried all during folk dancing. What if Mutt didn't eat it all up while the class was out of the room? But when they returned, Otis was relieved to find every crumb gone.

Friday was worst of all. Otis scarcely had time for breakfast, he was so anxious to get to school early. The door of Room Eleven was locked as usual, and there was no opportunity to slip food into the cage during the morning. By lunch time Otis was desperate. Even though he had not brought a sandwich for himself, he hid in the cloakroom again and took a chance that Stewy would not miss him. When the

43

classroom door was safely locked, he watched Mutt gobble the cheese he had brought him and look around for more. Hungry as he was, Otis gave the rat the rest of the cheese and a vitamin pill.

Suddenly Otis heard the sound of a key in the door. Mrs. Gitler was coming back! He looked frantically for a place to hide and made it to the cloakroom just as the classroom door opened. He crouched halfway between the cloakroom's two doors. Just to be safe, he pulled someone's raincoat over him. He heard Mrs. Gitler lock the classroom door from the inside. Then he heard her walk across the room, humming to herself.

Otis was afraid to move. He was almost afraid to breathe. Was she going to stay in the room for the whole lunch hour, for Pete's sake? He heard the drawer of her desk open. More humming. Then a snapping noise. What could that be? A compact, of course. Mrs. Gitler was powdering her nose.

Otis's left leg went to sleep. The drawer closed. A chair scraped. Mrs. Gitler walked down the side of the room by the windows. Would she . . . ? Yes, she did. She stopped by the rats' cages.

Otis's right leg went to sleep. If only he could be sure Mutt had finished the vitamin pill! He tried wiggling his toes inside his shoes to ease the numbness in his legs. Just then Mrs. Gitler started to walk toward the back of the room. Otis held his breath. He didn't know what he would do if she came into the cloakroom. He heard her pause at one of the cloakroom doors. Then she passed it. He was able to breathe again as he heard her open a cupboard, take something out, and close it again. If only she would leave the room!

Otis's hungry stomach began to rumble and then to growl. Frantically he pressed his arms against his middle. His stomach made an interesting gurgling noise. He squirmed silently. His stomach growled back at him. Surely it was loud enough for Mrs. Gitler to hear.

Mrs. Gitler's footsteps returned to the front of the room and Otis heard her sit down at her desk. He heard papers rustling and decided she was settled for the rest of the lunch period. At least she couldn't hear his noisy stomach from the front of the room.

Why did I ever think this was such a good idea anyway, thought Otis miserably. Maybe it wasn't such a good joke after all. Maybe the joke was really on him. Then he thought how close he was to rat-weighing time. No, he wouldn't give up. He would hang on a little longer. His legs felt as if they were stuck full of pins. Grimly he listened for each minute to click by on the electric clock. Each minute seemed so long he was sure the clock had stopped. Outside he heard the children laughing and shouting. He wondered if anyone missed him.

Finally, when Otis was sure he could not remain motionless another instant, the first bell rang and Mrs. Gitler unlocked the door. He waited until the halls were filled with noise before he came out from under the raincoat. Then he clung to a coat hook with one hand while he tried to make his stiff, prickly legs work.

Stewy was first into the cloakroom. He was eating a chocolate bar filled with almonds.

Otis had to swallow before he could say, "Hi."

"What are you doing here?" demanded Stewy suspiciously.

"I stayed in. I don't feel so good," said Otis, looking hungrily at the chocolate bar. And it was true. He couldn't think of a time when he had felt worse.

Stewy hung up his jacket, popped the rest of the chocolate into his mouth, and licked his fingers.

By that time Otis's feet were working once more and were able to carry him into the classroom. As he walked past the rats' cages he saw that the vitamin pill had disappeared, but he wondered uneasily what Mrs. Gitler had seen. He was glad his experiment was nearly at an end. He couldn't keep it up any longer. Not even for soda pop in the cafeteria.

When Monday morning finally arrived, Otis shoved his way through the excited boys and girls crowded around the rats. Sure enough, Mutt was bigger. Otis put his finger against the cage. With his whiskers quivering, Mutt put his front paws up on the wire and sniffed at Otis's finger. Good old Mutt, thought Otis. He knows me. He's just like my very own pet rat.

And then Otis began to wonder. What was going to happen to the rats when the experiment ended? Mutt was the only pet he had ever had. He was going to miss him when he was gone, unless . . . Maybe there was some way he could get to take Mutt home with him. Mrs. Brewster would not have to know about a pet rat, and Otis's mother was too busy to care.

Otis went to the teacher's desk. "Mrs. Gitler, what will happen to the rats when the experiment ends?" he asked.

"We'll talk about that when the time comes," she answered, and went on working on her lesson plans.

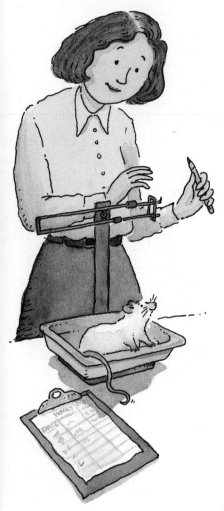

That only made Otis more anxious. After the class had taken their seats, he couldn't keep from watching Mutt. Such a fine healthy rat! And all because he had worked to make sure that he had good food. Otis had to find some way to keep him.

As Mrs. Gitler took the scales out of the cupboard, Otis still had not thought of a plan. He wished she would hurry as he watched her adjust the weights and set Pinky on the scale. She slid the weights back and forth some more before she said, "Pinky weighs one hundred and thirty grams." Then she lifted Mutt out of his cage, weighed him, and announced, "Mutt weighs one hundred and thirty-seven grams!"

Mutt was bigger than Pinky! Everyone began to talk at once.

"I have only one pair of ears," said Mrs. Gitler. "I can hear only one person at a time."

Secretly Otis felt that he had Mrs. Gitler in a pretty tight spot. He raised his hand and asked, "If Mutt grew more on white bread and soda pop than Pinky did on school lunches, doesn't that mean we should drink soda pop and eat white bread in the cafeteria?"

Soda pop in the cafeteria! Everyone had something to say.

Mrs. Gitler looked stern until the room was silent. Then she spoke quietly. "No, Otis, it does not mean that we should eat white bread and drink soda pop in the cafeteria." She paused to look sadly at the class. "It means that some boy or girl in this room has spoiled our experiment by feeding Mutt."

Otis stared at his teacher. Leave it to Mrs. Gitler to guess what had happened. Much as he disliked admitting it, even to himself, he had to admire her. You couldn't put anything over on Mrs. Gitler. At least, not very often. Otis squirmed uncomfortably. Poor Mrs. Gitler. How disappointed she looked — to think that one of her boys or girls would spoil the scientific experiment.

Now Otis did not know what to do. He had expected Mrs. Gitler to be surprised or maybe cross, not to look sad and disappointed. While Mrs. Gitler looked sadly at the class, Otis made up his mind to tell her what he had done. He would say he was sorry, and when Mrs. Gitler forgave him he would ask for Mutt.

But before he could get the words out, Ellen spoke. "Mrs. Gitler, I . . . I . . ." She gulped. Otis thought she sounded as if she was about to cry. "I fed Mutt. He . . . he looked so little and hungry that I felt sorry

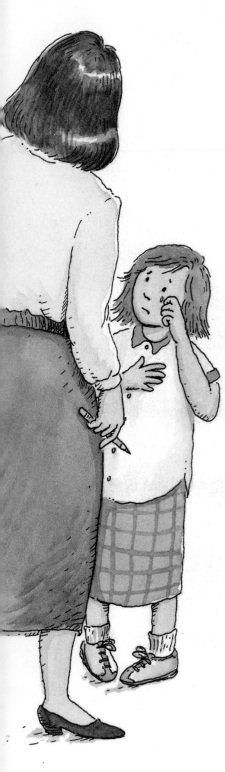

for him." She gulped again and looked miserably at Mrs. Gitler.

Otis stared at Ellen. Mrs. Gitler surprised him, but Ellen astounded him. Old Ellen Tebbits saying she fed Mutt just when he was going to tell what he had done. Well, he didn't believe it. It wasn't true. She couldn't have fed Mutt. Look at all the trouble he had had, trying to slip cheese and vitamin pills to him.

"How could you feed him without anybody seeing you?" Otis demanded.

"Yes, Ellen, and tell us what you fed him," said Mrs. Gitler.

"Every day I wrapped some of my lunch from the cafeteria in a paper napkin." Ellen paused to sniff unhappily. "And then I waited till everyone had gone home and then I asked the janitor to let me into the room for a minute. I didn't mean to spoil the experiment. Mutt just looked so . . . so hungry." Ellen burst into tears.

Now why didn't I think of that? thought Otis. That Ellen! He couldn't help feeling sorry for her, she looked so unhappy, but just the same . . . Mutt was his rat.

There was an embarrassed silence until Mrs. Gitler said briskly, "Even if the experiment didn't turn out as we planned, I'm sure we have all learned the important thing. That is, we must eat good food if we are to grow and be healthy."

That isn't what I learned, thought Otis. I learned you've got to be careful or some girl will get ahead of you.

Austine raised her hand. "Mrs. Gitler, if we aren't going on with the experiment, what is going to happen to Mutt and Pinky?"

"We'll find good homes for them," Mrs. Gitler answered. "Is there anyone who would like a pet rat?"

Otis waved his hand wildly, but Mrs. Gitler did not see him. She asked, "Who would like to take Pinky home?"

Otis stopped waving his hand. He wanted Mutt. The class finally decided Tommy should have Pinky. Stewy wanted him, but he already had a dog. Tommy, who had neither a dog nor a cat, could give a good home to a rat.

Now was Otis's chance. He waved his hand frantically. "Mrs. Gitler," he said. "Mrs. Gitler."

Otis knew she saw him, even though she said, "Yes, Ellen?"

Ellen twisted her handkerchief as she spoke. "I know I spoiled the experiment, but I'd like awfully much to take Mutt home. I sort of feel like he's my rat."

Otis didn't know what to do. He couldn't let Ellen have Mutt. He had to do something. "But I fed him too," he protested. "He's just as much mine as Ellen's. I went without my lunch to feed him." Otis watched Mrs. Gitler anxiously. She just had to see how important it was for him to have Mutt for his very own. He felt everyone staring at him. "Well, I did feed him," said Otis, when no one spoke. "And I gave him vitamin pills besides. He's just as much mine as he is Ellen's."

"Well, Otis, aren't you rather slow in telling us about this?" Mrs. Gitler looked stern, but Otis could see that behind her stern look she wanted to laugh.

This was no laughing matter to Otis. "I was going to tell, but Ellen beat me to it," he explained.

"Oh, I see," said Mrs. Gitler. "Yes, Ellen, since you told us about feeding Mutt first, you may have him for a pet."

"Aw, that's no fair," muttered Otis, trying to cover up his disappointment.

"What did you say, Otis?" asked Mrs. Gitler.

"Nothing." Otis scowled and slid down in his seat. That Ellen Tebbits! Taking his rat! Why, you wouldn't think a girl who was always neat and clean like Ellen would even like rats.

That afternoon Otis watched Mrs. Gitler put Mutt in a chalk box for Ellen to carry home. It seemed to him that he had never wanted anything as much as he wanted Mutt for his very own. Well, it was too late now. He took one last look at Mutt's bright eyes and quivering whiskers before he started home.

When Otis reached the apartment house he found Bucky, a kindergarten boy who lived in the same building, sitting on the front steps waiting for him. Although Otis didn't care much about playing with a five-year-old, he couldn't help liking Bucky, because he knew the little boy admired him and wanted to be like him when he grew up.

"Hi," said Bucky, who was wearing his cowboy suit. "Let's play like we're cowboys."

Otis sat down on the steps. "Not today," he said glumly, and began to pull a piece of rubber off the sole of his sneaker. He wished there was someone around to play with besides a little kindergartner. If only he had Mutt!

Then Otis looked down the street and saw Ellen coming toward him. She had changed to her play clothes and was carrying the chalk box. She looked unhappy.

"Hi," said Otis, wondering where she was going.

"Hello, Otis." Ellen stopped in front of the steps. "My mother says she won't have a rat in the house and I have to get rid of Mutt right away. I thought I'd give him to you, because you fed him and would take good care of him." She held out the chalk box.

Otis took it and slid back the lid to look at Mutt, who was cowering in a corner. "Gee . . ." said Otis. "Gee . . . thanks, Ellen." Gently he lifted Mutt out and stroked his soft white fur. Mutt snuggled into his hand. His very own Mutt!

"Could I come and see him sometimes?" Ellen asked timidly.

"Sure, any time." Otis decided Ellen wasn't so bad after all, even if she was always neat and clean and well behaved.

As Ellen left, Bucky began to chant, "Otis has a girl. Otis has a girl."

"You keep quiet," said Otis fiercely, "or I'll . . . I'll . . ."

"If you do anything to me, I'll tell the management on you," said Bucky.

"Well, keep quiet or I won't let you play with my rat," said Otis.

Bucky kept quiet.

Otis never has difficulty stirring up a little excitement. If you read the book *Otis Spofford,* you will learn just how much trouble Otis can get into.

Is It Fair?

Should Otis get to keep the rat after all? Form two groups to debate this issue. One group will give their arguments in favor of Otis's keeping Mutt. The other group will give arguments against. Join the group that shares your opinion. Then begin the debate, with the people in each group discussing their opinions.

From the book **Ramona Quimby, Age 8**

The Hard-boiled Egg FAD

Ramona Quimby, who once
caused so much trouble for
Henry Huggins, is growing up.
Now Ramona is eight years old,
in the third grade, and *still*
getting into trouble.

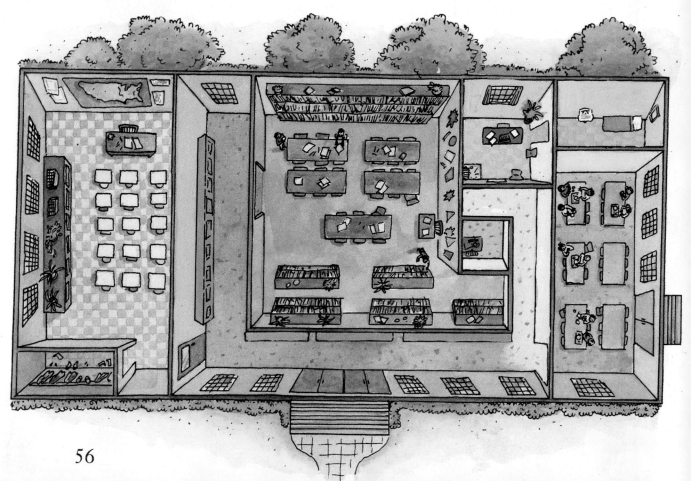

WITH ALL FOUR MEMBERS of the family leaving at different times in different directions, mornings were flurried in the Quimby household. On the days when Mr. Quimby had an eight o'clock class, he left early in the car. Beezus left next because she walked to school and because she wanted to stop for Mary Jane on the way.

Ramona was third to leave. She enjoyed these last few minutes alone with her mother now that Mrs. Quimby no longer reminded her she must be nice to Willa Jean.

"Did you remember to give me a hard-boiled egg in my lunch like I asked?" Ramona inquired one morning. This week hard-boiled eggs were popular with third-graders, a fad started by Yard Ape, who sometimes brought his lunch. Last week the fad had been individual bags of corn chips. Ramona had been left out of that fad because her mother objected to spending money on junk food. Surely her mother would not object to a nutritious hard-boiled egg.

"Yes, I remembered the hard-boiled egg, you little rabbit," said Mrs. Quimby. "I'm glad you have finally learned to like them."

Ramona did not feel it necessary to explain to her mother that she still did not like hard-boiled eggs, not even when they had been dyed for Easter. Neither did she like soft-boiled eggs, because she did not like slippery, slithery food. Ramona liked deviled eggs, but deviled eggs were not the fad, at least not this week.

On the bus Ramona and Susan compared lunches. Each was happy to discover that the other had a hard-boiled egg, and both were eager for lunchtime to come.

While Ramona waited for lunch period, school turned out to be unusually interesting. After the class had filled out their arithmetic workbooks, Mrs. Whaley handed each child a glass jar containing about two inches of a wet blue substance — she explained that it was oatmeal dyed blue. Ramona was first to say "Yuck." Most people made faces, and Yard Ape made a gagging noise.

"OK, kids, quiet down," said Mrs. Whaley. When the room was quiet, she explained that for science they were going to study fruit flies. The blue oatmeal contained fruit-fly larvae. "And why do you think the oatmeal is blue?" she asked.

Several people thought the blue dye was some sort of food for the larvae, vitamins maybe. Marsha suggested the oatmeal was dyed blue so the children wouldn't think it was good to eat. Everybody laughed at this guess. Who would ever think cold oatmeal was good to eat? Yard Ape came up with the right answer: the oatmeal was dyed blue so the larvae could be seen. And so they could — little white specks.

As the class bent over their desks making labels for their jars, Ramona wrote her name on her slip of paper and added, "Age 8," which she always wrote after her signature. Then she drew tiny fruit flies around it before she pasted the label on her very own jar of blue oatmeal and fruit-fly larvae. Now she had a jar of pets.

"That's a really neat label, Ramona," said Mrs. Whaley. Ramona understood that her teacher did not mean tidy when she said "neat," but extra good. Ramona decided she liked Mrs. Whaley after all.

The morning was so satisfactory that it passed quickly. When lunchtime came,

Ramona collected her lunch box and went off to the cafeteria where, after waiting in line for her milk, she sat at a table with Sara, Janet, Marsha, and other third-grade girls. She opened her lunch box, and there, tucked in a paper napkin, snug between her sandwich and an orange, was her hard-boiled egg, smooth and perfect, the right size to fit her hand. Because Ramona wanted to save the best for the last, she ate the center of her sandwich — tuna fish — and poked a hole in her orange so she could suck out the juice. Third-graders did not peel their oranges. At last it was time for the egg.

There were a number of ways of cracking eggs. The most popular, and the real reason for bringing an egg to school, was knocking the egg against one's head. There were two ways of doing so, by a lot of timid little raps or by one big whack.

Sara was a rapper. Ramona, like Yard Ape, was a whacker. She took a firm hold on her egg, waited until everyone at her table was watching, and *whack* — she found herself with a handful of crumbled shell and something cool and slimy running down her face.

Everyone at Ramona's table gasped. Ramona needed a moment to realize what had happened. Her egg was raw. Her mother had

not boiled her egg at all. She tried to brush the yellow yolk and slithery white out of her hair and away from her face, but she only succeeded in making her hands eggy. Her eyes filled with tears of anger, which she tried to brush away with her wrists. The gasps at her table turned into giggles. From another table, Ramona caught a glimpse of Yard Ape grinning at her.

Marsha, a tall girl who always tried to be motherly, said, "It's all right, Ramona. I'll take you to the bathroom and help you wash off the egg."

Ramona was not one bit grateful. "You go away," she said, ashamed of being so rude. She did not want this third-grade girl treating her like a baby.

The teacher who was supervising lunch period came over to see what the commotion was about. Marsha gathered up all the paper napkins from the lunch boxes at the table and handed them to the teacher, who tried to sop up the egg. Unfortunately, the napkins did not absorb egg very well. Instead, they smeared yolk and white around in Ramona's hair. Her face felt stiff as egg white began to dry.

"Take her to the office," the teacher said to Marsha. "Mrs. Larson will help her."

"Come on, Ramona," said Marsha, as if Ramona were in kindergarten. She put her hand on Ramona's shoulder because Ramona's hands were too eggy to touch.

Ramona jerked away. "I can go by myself." With that reply, she ran out of the cafeteria. She was so angry she was able to ignore the giggles and the few sympathetic looks of the other children. Ramona was mad at herself for following a fad. She was furious with Yard Ape for grinning at her. Most of all she was angry with her mother for not boiling the egg in the first place. By the time she reached the office, Ramona's face felt as stiff as a mask.

Ramona almost ran into Mr. Wittman, the principal, which would have upset her even more. He was someone Ramona always tried to avoid ever since Beezus had told her that the way to remember how to spell the kind of principal who was the principal of a school was to remember the word ended in *p-a-l,* not *p-l-e,* because the principal was her pal. Ramona did not want the principal to be her pal. She wanted him to mind his own business, aloof and important, in his office. Mr. Wittman must have felt the same way because he stepped — almost jumped — quickly aside.

Mrs. Larson, the school secretary, took one look at Ramona, sprang from her desk, and said, "Well, you need a little help, don't you?"

Ramona nodded, grateful to Mrs. Larson for behaving as if eggy third-graders walked into her office every day. The secretary led her into a tiny room equipped with a cot, washbasin, and toilet that adjoined the office.

"Let's see," said Mrs. Larson, "how shall we go about this? I guess the best way is to wash your hands, then dunk your head. You've heard of egg shampoos, haven't you? They are supposed to be wonderful for the hair."

"Yow!" yelped Ramona, when she dipped her head into the washbasin. "The water's cold."

"It's probably a good thing we don't have warmer water," said Mrs. Larson. "You wouldn't want to cook the egg in your

hair, would you?" She rubbed and Ramona
snuffled. She rinsed and Ramona sniffed.
Finally Mrs. Larson said, "That's the best I can
do," and handed Ramona a wad of paper towels.
"Dry yourself off the best you can," she said.
"You can wash your hair when you get home."

Ramona accepted the towels. As she sat on
the cot, rubbing and blotting and seething in
humiliation and anger, she listened to sounds
from the office, the click of the typewriter, the
ring of the telephone, Mrs. Larson's voice
answering.

Ramona began to calm down and feel a
little better. Maybe Mrs. Kemp would let her
wash her hair after school. She could let Willa
Jean pretend to be working in a beauty shop
and not say anything about her Sustained Silent
Reading. One of these days Willa Jean was sure
to catch on that she was just reading a book,
and Ramona wanted to postpone that time as
long as possible.

Toward the end of lunch period, Ramona heard teachers drift into the office to leave papers or pick up messages from their boxes. Then Ramona made an interesting discovery. Teachers talked about their classes.

"My class has been so good today," said one teacher. "I can hardly believe it. They're little angels."

"I don't know what's the matter with my class today," said another. "Yesterday they knew how to subtract, and today none of them seems able to remember."

"Perhaps it's the weather," suggested another teacher.

Ramona found all this conversation most interesting. She had blotted her hair as best she could when she heard Mrs. Whaley's big cheerful voice speaking to Mrs. Larson. "Here are those tests I was supposed to hand in yesterday," she said. "Sorry I'm late." Mrs. Larson murmured an answer.

Then Mrs. Whaley said, "I hear my little show-off came in with egg in her hair." She laughed and added, "What a nuisance."

Ramona was so stunned she did not try to hear Mrs. Larson's answer. Show-off! Nuisance! Did Mrs. Whaley think she had broken a raw egg into her hair on purpose to show off? And to be called a nuisance by her teacher when she was not a nuisance. Or was she? Ramona did not mean to break an egg in her hair. Her mother was to blame. Did this accident make her a nuisance?

Ramona did not see why Mrs. Whaley could think she was a nuisance when Mrs. Whaley was not the one to get her hands all eggy. Yet Ramona had heard her say right out loud that she was a show-off and a nuisance. That hurt, really hurt.

Ramona sat as still as she could with the damp paper towels in her hands. She did not want to risk even the softest noise by throwing them into the wastebasket. Lunch period came to an end, and still she sat. Her body felt numb and so did her heart. She could never, never face Mrs. Whaley again. Never.

Mrs. Larson's typewriter clicked cheerfully away. Ramona was forgotten, which was the way she wanted it. She even wanted to forget herself and her horrible hair, now drying into stiff spikes. She no longer felt like a real person.

The next voice Ramona heard was that of Yard Ape. "Mrs. Larson," he said, as if he had been running in the hall, "Mrs. Whaley said to tell you Ramona didn't come back after lunch."

The typing stopped. "Oh, my goodness," said Mrs. Larson, as she appeared in the doorway. "Why, Ramona, are you still here?"

How was Ramona supposed to answer?

"Run along back to class with Danny," said the secretary. "I'm sorry I forgot all about you."

"Do I have to?" asked Ramona.

"Of course," said Mrs. Larson. "Your hair is almost dry. You don't want to miss class."

Ramona did want to miss class. Forever. The third grade was spoiled forever.

"Aw, come on, Ramona," said Yard Ape, for once not teasing.

Surprised by sympathy from Yard Ape, Ramona reluctantly left the office. She expected him to go on ahead of her, but instead he walked beside her, as if they were friends instead of rivals. Ramona felt strange walking down the hall alone with a boy. As she trudged along beside him, she felt she had to tell someone the terrible news. "Mrs. Whaley doesn't like me," she said in a flat voice.

"Don't let old Whaley get you down," he answered. "She likes you OK. You're a good kid."

Ramona was a little shocked at hearing her teacher called "old Whaley." However, she squeezed comfort from Yard Ape's opinion. She began to like him, really like him.

When they reached their classroom, Yard Ape, perhaps thinking he had been *too* nice to Ramona, turned and said to her with his old grin, "Egghead!"

Oh! There was nothing for Ramona to do but follow him into the room. Sustained Silent Reading, or DEAR, as Mrs. Whaley called it, was over, and class was practicing writing cursive capital letters. Mrs. Whaley was describing capital *M* as she wrote it on the board. "Swoop down, swoop up, down, up again, and down." Ramona avoided looking at her teacher as she got out paper and pencil and began to write the capital letters of the alphabet in careful, even script. She enjoyed the work, and it soothed her hurt feelings until she came to the letter *Q*.

Ramona sat looking at the cursive capital *Q*, the first letter of her last name. Ramona had always been fond of *Q*, the only letter of the alphabet with a neat little tail. She enjoyed printing *Q*, but she did not like her written *Q*.

She had made it right, but it looked like a big floppy 2, which Ramona felt was a dumb way to make such a nice letter.

Ramona decided right then and there that she would never again write a cursive *Q*. She would write the rest of her last name, *uimby*, in cursive, but she would always, no matter what Mrs. Whaley said, print her capital *Q*'s.

So there, Mrs. Whaley, thought Ramona. You can't make me write a cursive *Q* if I don't want to. She began to feel like a real person again.

Getting a little egg on her face is only one of the funny episodes in Ramona's life. The book *Ramona Quimby, Age 8* tells all about Ramona's further mishaps in the third grade.

What's Hot, What's Not

Strange haircuts. The latest basketball sneaker. New brands of blue jeans. All these could be fads at your school. Fads come and go, just like hard-boiled eggs and bags of corn chips at Ramona's school.

With a group of classmates, make a mural of the fads at your school. Cut out magazine pictures or draw your own pictures of "what's hot" and "what's not." Set them up on a bulletin board in two categories so that they make a mural.

Meet Some New Authors

Johanna Hurwitz and Carol and Donald Carrick
are other authors who have created characters like
Otis, Henry, and Ramona. Here are some of their
books, along with one by Beverly Cleary.

Ramona Quimby, Age 8
by Beverly Cleary
Ramona is back with a new school and
a new teacher. Best of all, she gets
to ride the bus to school all alone.

Class Clown *by Johanna Hurwitz*
Lucas loves to have fun in class.
Only his kind of fun usually gets
him in trouble.

Aldo Applesauce *by Johanna Hurwitz*
When Aldo Sossi spills applesauce on his first day at his new school, he gets the nickname Aldo Applesauce. Moving to a new town has never been so difficult.

Sleep Out *by Carol and Donald Carrick*
Christopher wants to try out the new sleeping bag that he got for his birthday. But a night alone in the woods can be very scary.

The Foundling
by Carol and Donald Carrick
Christopher's dog Bodger was killed by a pickup truck weeks ago. How will Christopher ever replace his best friend?

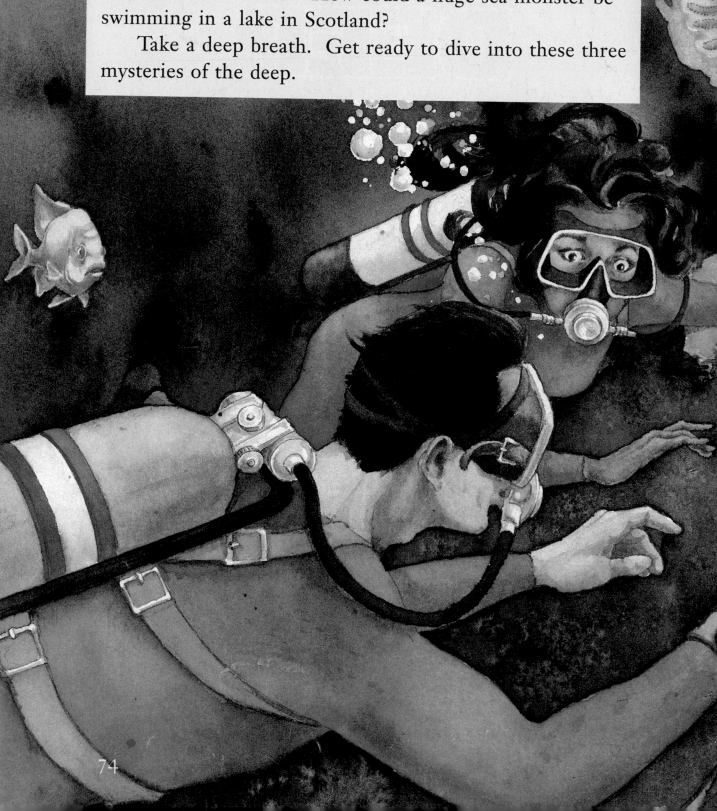

Deep beneath the waters lie mysteries so puzzling, people have wondered about them for years. How could a ship that was supposed to be unsinkable actually go down on its first voyage? How could a fish that scientists thought was extinct for centuries suddenly appear off the coast of South Africa? How could a huge sea monster be swimming in a lake in Scotland?

Take a deep breath. Get ready to dive into these three mysteries of the deep.

CONTENTS

THE TITA

Lost...

NIC

and Found

BY JUDY DONNELLY

1. The Wonder Ship

It is April 10, 1912.

The whole world is talking about an amazing new ship. Its name is the *Titanic*.

The ship is getting ready to leave on its first trip across the ocean. It is going all the way from England to America.

Newspapers call the *Titanic* "The Wonder Ship." They say it is like a floating palace. The *Titanic* has restaurants, a post office — even a gym with a toy camel to ride.

The picture on page 79 shows the ship as if it were sliced open. The fancy rooms are on the top decks. On the lowest deck you can see the squash court and the swimming pool.

The *Titanic* is the biggest ship the world has ever seen. The ship is almost four city blocks long and is as tall as an eleven-story building.

Best of all, experts say the *Titanic* is the safest ship ever. They say it cannot sink. Why? The ship doesn't have one bottom — it has two. One is inside the other.

The **Titanic** *sets sail.*   *The ship's engines ran on huge boilers like these.*

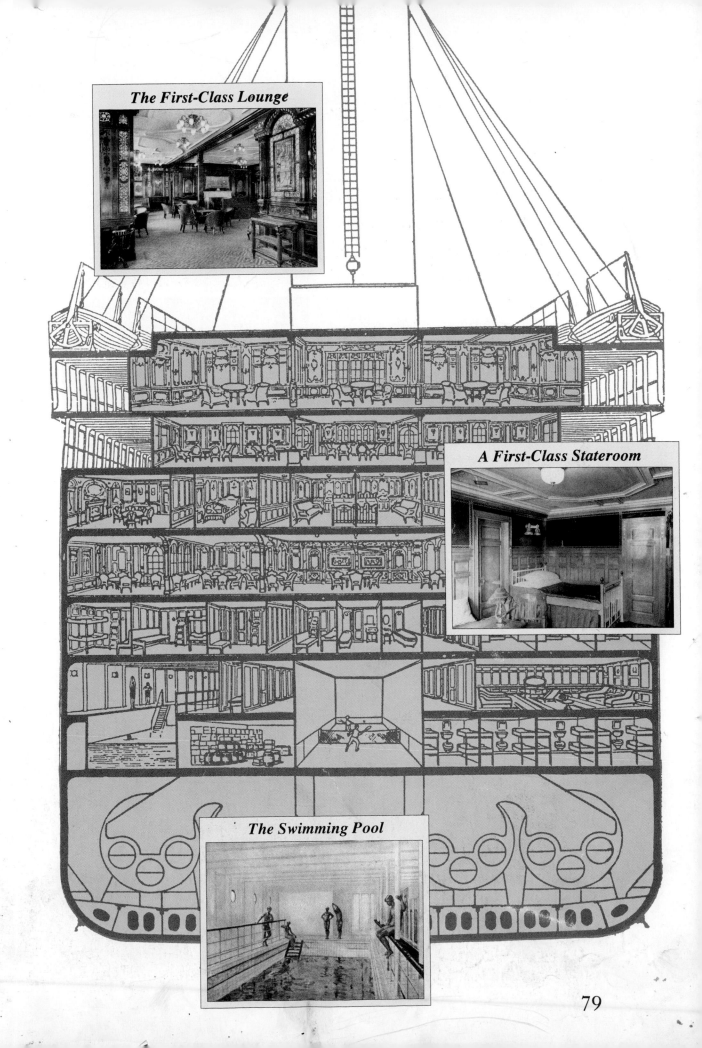

The First-Class Lounge

A First-Class Stateroom

The Swimming Pool

79

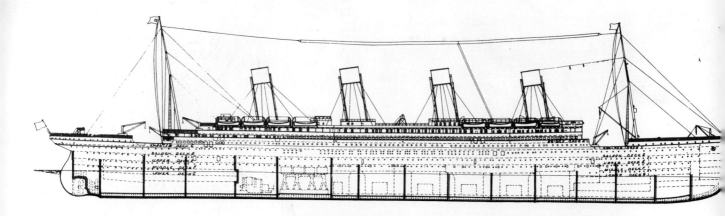

The drawing above shows the watertight compartments in the bottom, or **hull**, *of the* Titanic. *The drawing on the right shows a thick steel door to one of the* Titanic's *watertight compartments.*

The lowest part of the *Titanic* is divided into sixteen watertight compartments. If one compartment starts to flood, the captain can just pull a switch. A thick steel door will shut. The water will be trapped. It cannot flood the rest of the ship. Two or three or even four compartments can be full of water. Still, the *Titanic* will float.

The *Titanic* has another nickname — "The Rich Man's Special." Some of the richest people in the world are sailing on the *Titanic*. Their tickets cost more money than a sailor earns in a lifetime.

Not all the passengers are rich. Some have very little money. They are not traveling for fun. They are going off to find a new home in America.

At last the big moment comes. The *Titanic* is ready to sail!

Crowds line the shore. Flags wave. A band is playing.

Passengers come out on the decks. They wave good-bye to their friends.

The engines roar. Slowly the ship steams out of the harbor. The *Titanic* has begun its first voyage.

No one guesses this will also be its last.

2. Iceberg

It is April 14, 1912. The *Titanic* is in icy waters off the coast of Canada.

It is almost midnight. The ship is quiet. The sea is smooth as glass. The air is biting cold.

The passengers have had a good dinner. Some of them are still up playing cards. Most are asleep in their rooms.

It is a good night to be inside. But the lookout must watch for danger. He is high above the ship in the crow's-nest. He stares into the darkness.

Suddenly the lookout sees a dark shape. It is a mountain of ice! And the *Titanic* is heading right into it! The lookout rings an alarm. He calls, "Iceberg straight ahead!"

A seaman is below, steering the ship. He tries to turn the ship away. But it is too late.

The giant iceberg scrapes along the side of the ship.

There is a bump. A grinding noise. It doesn't seem like much. Some people do not even notice.

But the captain hurries from his room. He goes down below. He wants to see if the ship is hurt. Soon he learns the terrible truth.

The iceberg has hurt the ship badly. Water is pouring in. Five of the watertight compartments are already flooded. And that is too many. Nothing can be done now.

It seems impossible. But it is true. The *Titanic* is going to sink!

This message (above right) warned of icebergs, but Captain Edward Smith (above) doubted his ship was in danger. Later, the ship radioed for help from a room like this (right).

The captain gives his orders. Wake the passengers! Radio for help! And make the lifeboats ready!

The captain is afraid. He knows that 2,227 people are on board. And there are only enough lifeboats for 1,100 of them.

The passengers do not know this. As people come out on deck, they laugh and joke. Some are in evening gowns. Others wear life jackets over pajamas. But they are not worried. They still think they are on a ship that cannot sink.

Get in the lifeboats, the sailors tell them. Women and children go first. Men go only if there is room.

Many do not want to get in. The big ship seems so safe. The little lifeboats do not.

The sailors are in a hurry. They know there is trouble. They rush people into the lifeboats. Some are only half full, but the sailors lower them anyway.

Many passengers are far from the lifeboats. They are the poor ones. Their rooms are down below. They know there is trouble too. But they do not know where to go. A few try to find their way. They go up stairs and down halls. Some are helped by seamen. Most just wait below.

In the radio room the operator calls for help. Other ships answer. But they are many, many miles away.

One ship is not far away. Its name is the *Californian*. This ship is only ten miles from the *Titanic*. It could reach the sinking ship in minutes and save everyone.

The *Titanic*'s operator calls again and again. But the *Californian* does not answer. It is late at night and the ship's radio is turned off. No one on board hears the calls for help.

The *Titanic* tries to signal the *Californian*. It sets off rockets that look like fireworks. Sailors on the *Californian* see the rockets. But they do not understand that the *Titanic* is in trouble. And so they do not come.

On the *Titanic* the band is playing. The music is cheerful. But people are afraid now. The deck is slanting under their feet.

The ship tilts more and more. The lower decks are underwater.

Two lifeboats are left, but the sailors cannot get them loose. Hundreds and hundreds of people are still on board. And by now they know the end is near.

An old couple holds hands. The wife will not leave her husband. One man puts on his best clothes. "I will die like a gentleman," he says.

Some people jump into the icy water. A few are lucky. They reach a lifeboat.

The people in the lifeboats row away from the *Titanic*. Everyone is staring at the beautiful ship. Its

lights are sparkling. The lively music drifts across
the water.

   Then the music changes. The band plays a hymn.

   One end of the huge ship slides slowly into the ocean.
The music stops. There is a great roaring noise. A
million sparks fill the air. The other end of the ship
swings straight up.

   For a moment the *Titanic* stays pointed at the stars.
Then it disappears under the black water.

3. Never Again

It is 2:20 A.M. on April 15.

The *Titanic* is gone.

The people in the lifeboats stare into the night. The sky is full of shooting stars. But it is dark. And it is bitter, bitter cold.

Most of the lifeboats have drifted away from each other.

People just wait. And they try to get warm. Some have fur coats. Others are wearing bathrobes and slippers. One man is in nothing but his underwear. Coldest of all are the ones who jumped from the ship and swam to a boat. Their hair and clothes are frosted with ice.

One lifeboat is upside down. About thirty men are standing on it. They lean this way and that to keep the boat from sinking. Icy waves splash against their legs.

One lifeboat goes back to try and help. They save one man. He is floating on a wooden door. They do not find many others. No one can last long in the freezing water.

Hours pass. The sky grows lighter. It seems as if help will never come. Then suddenly a light flashes. And another. It is a ship — the *Carpathia*. It has come from fifty-eight miles away.

Everyone waves and cheers. They make torches. They burn paper, handkerchiefs — anything. They want to make the ship see them.

The sun begins to rise. There are icebergs all around. The rescue ship almost hits one, but it turns just in time. The ship keeps heading toward the lifeboats.

Help has finally come.

All eyes are on the rescue ship. Boat by boat, the people are taken aboard. The sea is rough and it takes many hours. But at last everyone is safe.

Soon the news flashes all around the world. The unsinkable *Titanic* has sunk. More than 2,200 people set out. Only 705 are rescued.

How? Why? No one can understand.

When the rescue ship reaches New York, forty thousand people are waiting. The *Titanic* survivors tell their stories.

The world learns the truth. The safest ship was not safe at all.

It was too late for the *Titanic*. But it was not too late for other ships.

New safety laws were passed. Many changes were made.

Today every ship must have enough lifeboats for every single passenger. And every ship has lifeboat drills so people know what to do if there is an accident.

Ship radios can never be turned off. Every call for help is heard.

And now there is a special ice patrol. Patrol airplanes keep track of dangerous icebergs. They warn ships. Never again can an iceberg take a ship by surprise.

The *Titanic* was a terrible loss. But the world learned from it.

4. Found at Last

Years went by. The *Titanic* lay many miles down in black, icy cold water.

No divers could go down in such deep water. And no one could even find the ship. The map above shows you roughly where the *Titanic* sank.

Some people thought the *Titanic* had been crushed. They said it was probably in a million pieces.

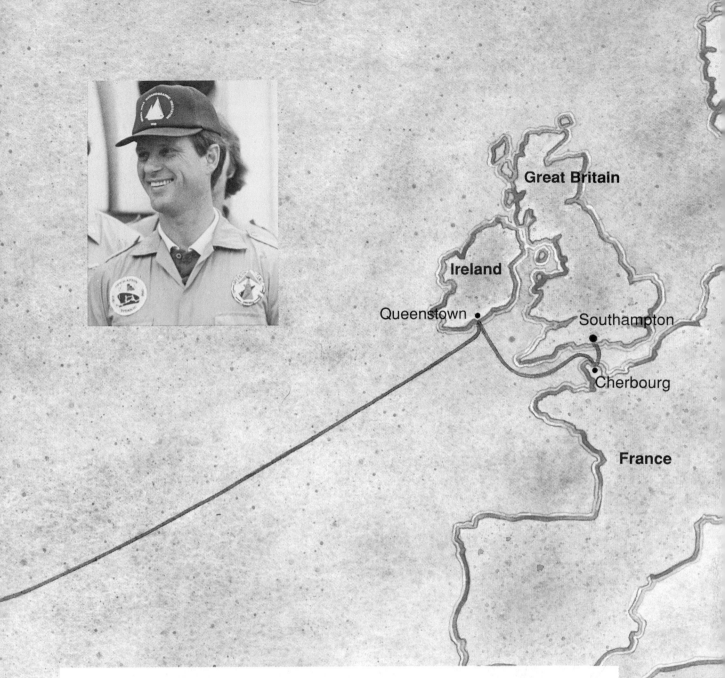

Great Britain

Ireland

Queenstown

Southampton

Cherbourg

France

Yet treasure hunters kept on dreaming of the wonderful ship. They were sure there was gold on board — and diamonds and pearls.

A man named Robert Ballard dreamed of the *Titanic* too. Robert was a scientist. He studied the oceans.

Robert worked in a famous laboratory in Woods Hole, Massachusetts. He didn't care about treasure. He just wanted to find the ship. He thought about it for years.

Robert had a special invention. It was a kind of underwater robot. Its name was Argo.

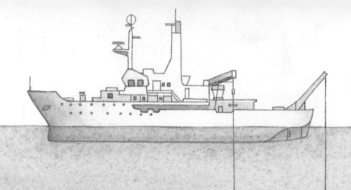

Argo could dive down very, very deep. It had lights and a video camera. It could skim along the ocean floor. It could take underwater video pictures. And it could send them to TV screens on a ship.

Robert read all about the *Titanic*. He looked at maps and photos. Finally he was ready. He thought he knew where the mystery ship was waiting.

In the summer of 1985, Robert sailed north to Newfoundland. He went with a team of scientists. He took Argo with them.

This drawing shows the underwater robot **Argo** *with other scientific equipment used to find the wreck of the* **Titanic.**

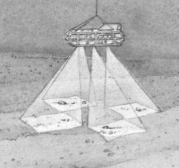

Robert sent Argo hunting. He didn't even have to get his feet wet. But he had to do a lot of watching. For days it was the same. He saw sand and more sand.

Then at last something different flashed on the screen. Was it a ship? Yes, it was. A huge ship.

The other scientists began to cheer. They had done it. They had found the *Titanic*!

Robert Ballard looking at video pictures sent by **Argo**. *The picture at left shows* **Argo** *out of the water.*

Robert could not believe his eyes. It was like seeing a ghost. There was the *Titanic*, sitting on the ocean floor. It had broken apart. But Robert could see how beautiful it still was.

Over the days Robert saw more and more of the ship. He saw the crow's-nest where the lookout first spotted the iceberg. A beautiful glass window lay in the sand. The ship's giant anchors were there. Bottles of wine were scattered about. And suitcases.

It was amazing. And it was sad. So many people had
set out on the voyage. So few had returned.

Finally Robert sailed home. He did not tell anyone
where he found the *Titanic*. He hoped the ship would stay
just as it was. He did not want treasure hunters to come
and loot it.

Robert wanted to go back to the *Titanic*. And a year later he did. He landed a small submarine right on the deck of the *Titanic*. He sent a robot inside the ship.

Robert did not take anything. But he did leave something behind. It was a message. He left it for anyone else who might find the *Titanic*. He asked that the great ship be left in peace.

All over the world people were thrilled by Robert's work. To some, it was very special. They had sailed on the *Titanic*.

They had been small children then. Now they were very old.

But they had never forgotten the "unsinkable *Titanic*." The world would never forget.

What's Down There?

Robert Ballard amazed the world with his discovery of the *Titanic* on the floor of the Atlantic Ocean. Pretend you are a reporter at Ballard's first news conference. What will you ask him? Write five questions to ask Ballard about the *Titanic*.

The Long-Lost Coelacanth

from *The Long-Lost Coelacanth
and Other Living Fossils*
written and illustrated by Aliki

One December day in 1938, a fisherman in South
Africa caught a strange fish. The fisherman had fished all
his life. But he had never seen a fish like this one.

The fish was almost five feet long. It was a beautiful
deep blue. It was covered with large scales. The strangest
parts of the fish were its fins. They did not lie flat the
way most fins do. They sprouted out of its body like
paddles.

Little did the fisherman know that he had caught a
wonderful present for scientists all over the world.

When scientists heard about the fish, they could not believe their ears. They knew there had been fish like this 70 million years ago. But they thought such fish had disappeared. They thought they were extinct. Yet, here was one of those ancient fish. The fisherman had caught a COELACANTH!

102

PLEISTOCENE	0-1 million years ago	ice ages	MAN
TERTIARY	1-63 million years ago		MODERN PLANTS
CRETACEOUS	63-135 million yrs. ago	sea dragon Tylosaurus	flying reptile Pteranodon giant birds
JURASSIC	135-181 million yrs. ago		
TRIASSIC	181-230 million yrs. ago	fishlike reptiles	DINOSAURS
PERMIAN	230-280 million yrs. ago	REPTILES	
CARBONIFEROUS	280-345 million yrs. ago	fern	moss INSECTS
DEVONIAN	340-405 million yrs. ago	RHIPIDISTIAN	COELACANTH EARLY F
SILURIAN	405-425 million yrs. ago	land plant	
ORDOVICIAN	425-500 million yrs. ago	CLAM	naut TRI
CAMBRIAN	500-600 million yrs. ago	starfish scorpion crinoid	
PRE-CAMBRIAN	600-? million yrs. ago	algae seaweed	

Scientists knew about coelacanths. They had found
fossils of ancient coelacanths buried in stone. Sometimes,
when a coelacanth died, it was covered with mud. In time,
the mud became as hard as stone. The fish became as
hard as stone, too. It became a fossil.

Scientists had studied coelacanth fossils. They knew
the fish lived long ago.
They knew it was one
of the first creatures
to have a backbone.

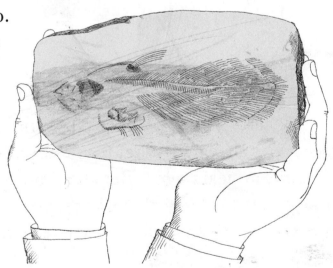

PTERANODON

DINOSAUR
(Triceratops)

Many creatures that were living long ago have died out. There are no live trilobites or nautiloids, pteranodons or dinosaurs. They are all extinct. We can tell what they looked like because we have found fossils of them.

But some kinds of early animals and plants did not die out. They did not become extinct. We call them "living fossils" because they look very much like their ancestors, which lived millions of years ago.

TRILOBITE

NAUTILOID

Now a coelacanth had been found alive! How excited the whole world was when the new "living fossil" was discovered. People read about it in the newspapers. Scientists knew there must be more coelacanths. They put up posters, and offered a big reward to any fisherman who caught another one.

Fishermen fished and fished. They looked and looked. Even divers searched for coelacanths.

It took fourteen years to find another coelacanth. Later, more were found. About thirty coelacanths have been fished out of the sea.

CROSSOPTERYGIANS

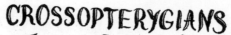
(means "fringe fin")

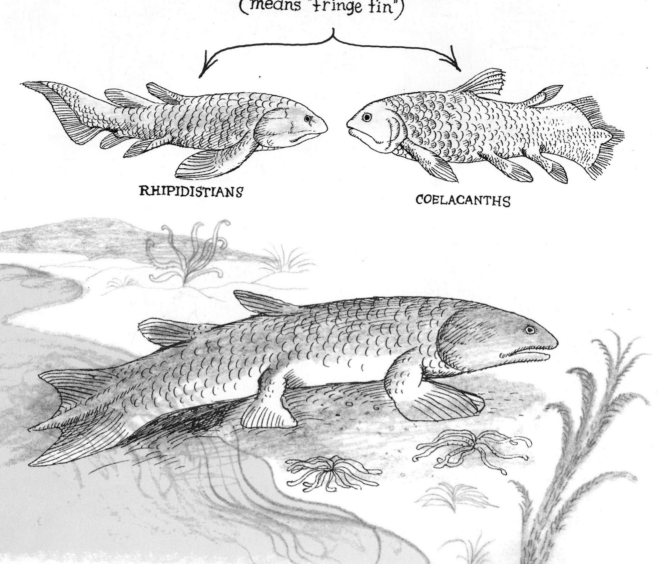

RHIPIDISTIANS

COELACANTHS

Now scientists were able to study the fish and learn more about it. They learned more about the past.

The coelacanth is a fish in the family of crossopterygians. Crossopterygians are different from all other fish. They are the only fish with fins like paddles. There are two groups of crossopterygians — the coelacanths and the rhipidistians.

Scientists knew that when land began to form, some ancient fish grew legs. The fish learned to breathe air, and to walk on dry land. Scientists now know that the paddles of the crossopterygians were the start of legs.

The rhipidistians grew into the first amphibians. Amphibians are animals that live on land as well as water. Frogs and toads are amphibians.

But the coelacanth never lived on dry land. It stayed in the water. Its fins did not turn into legs. The coelacanth looks just the way it did millions of years ago. Only today it is bigger.

To learn more about other living fossils, you may want to read the rest of The Long-Lost Coelacanth and Other Living Fossils *by Aliki.*

TO FISH OR NOT TO FISH

Should more
coelacanths be
caught for scientists
to study, or should
coelacanths be left alone
in the sea? What do you
think? Discuss this issue
with a group of classmates.

M

Wh
shaped
All
underwa
Cor
world.
the Red

1. Spong
wrasse (r

1.

Until I Saw the Sea

Until I saw the sea
I did not know
that wind
could wrinkle water so.

I never knew
that sun
could splinter a whole sea of blue.

Nor
did I know before,
a sea breathes in and out
upon a shore.

Lilian Moore

112

Sea Shell

Sea Shell, Sea Shell,
Sing me a song, O please!
A song of ships, and sailor men,
And parrots, and tropical trees,

Of islands lost in the Spanish Main
Which no man ever may find again,
Of fishes and corals under the waves,
And sea horses stabled in great green caves.

Sea Shell, Sea Shell,
Sing of the things you know so well.

Amy Lowell

113

THE Loch Ness Monster

BY ELLEN RABINOWICH

If you met a monster, what would you do? Most people would probably scream and run, but they would love to see a monster from a distance. Monsters have fascinated people for hundreds of years. Some people believe that monsters are real. Others don't.

This book is about the most famous monster in the world. Maybe it will help you decide what to think about monsters.

Monsters are often thought of as big, frightening creatures that scientists can't explain. Some people think that prehistoric animals were monsters. These animals were giant reptiles that lived long before people. The dinosaur was one prehistoric animal.

A frightening monster in fairy tales is the dragon. In stories its sharp claws can tear a person to pieces, and its hot breath can burn a person to a crisp. However, scientists know that no real animal can breathe fire. The dragon is a make-believe monster.

For hundreds of years people all over the world have said they have seen real monsters. Some are thought to live in oceans and lakes. Others are said to haunt forests. Many children believe that monsters visit their bedrooms at night. These, of course, aren't real.

Sometimes monsters turn out to be real animals that we know. Long ago, many sailors were afraid of the sea.

116

They were afraid that sea serpents or monsters would attack their ships. Sometimes, these monsters turned out to be strange, large animals like the octopus or giant squid. At other times, these monsters stayed a mystery.

One mysterious monster is so famous that it has often made newspaper headlines. Some people have left their jobs, homes, and families to look for this monster. Several British politicians thought this monster so important that they talked about it in Parliament. And three American astronauts asked to hear what these politicians were saying as their spaceship, the *Apollo 11*, raced toward the moon.

This monster has a name. It is called the Loch Ness Monster.

In the Scottish Highlands, there is a deep, dark lake called Loch Ness. (Loch is the Scottish word for "lake.") Tall pine trees surround it, and on one shore the spooky ruins of Urquhart Castle loom. There is something very

117

frightening about this lake. Thousands of people say they have seen a monster rise out of it.

The Scottish have given their famous Loch Ness Monster a name. They call her Nessie.

What does Nessie look like? No one knows for sure. Some people say she has a long neck like a giraffe with small horns on her head. Others say that she has humps like a camel. Still others say she's over 40 feet (12 m) long, with flippers like a seal. Only on one point does everyone agree. Nessie doesn't look like anything they have ever seen.

People have also seen Nessie doing strange things. They say:

She streaks beneath the water like a torpedo.
She trails a sizzling wake of white foam.
She showers spray in all directions
    when she surfaces.
She sinks back into the water straight down
    like a stone.

Also, Nessie is not only a water monster! She has been spotted several times on land!

For years, there have been frightening stories about Nessie. Most people are just afraid when they see her. But sometimes Nessie makes people fear for their lives.

One story is about three fishermen. Late one night they set out in a small boat looking for salmon. Loch Ness is a fine lake for fishing. It is full of salmon, eel, pike, and trout. But these fishermen were breaking the law. No fishing is allowed in Loch Ness after eight at night.

It was a beautiful spring night. The men were sure they would catch lots of fish. Suddenly, they forgot about fishing. Something very big was under their boat. And that something was lifting them up and out of the water. The men went white with fright. What strange force could do this? Then, suddenly their boat came back down. The men saw a giant shape swim away. Was it Nessie? The men didn't know. But they did know they would never break the law again.

Could Nessie really be a monster? Are such creatures real? One Dutch scientist, Dr. Bernard Heuvelmans, says "Yes." Dr. Heuvelmans is different from most scientists. He believes that the giant creatures called sea serpents that frightened sailors were, in fact, real and he believes Nessie is one of them.

Some scientists believe that Nessie isn't a monster at all. They think she might be some kind of mammal that we know about, like the sea cow or otter. Near Alaska, one kind of sea cow grew to 35 feet (10.6 m).

However, other scientists believe differently. They are sure that this giant kind of sea cow died out years ago. Also, sea cows don't have long necks like Nessie and must surface to breathe. If Nessie breathed air like other mammals, she would probably be seen more often.

In 1972 scientists at Loch Ness used an underwater camera to take this photograph. They believed the photograph showed a flipper from a 30–foot creature.

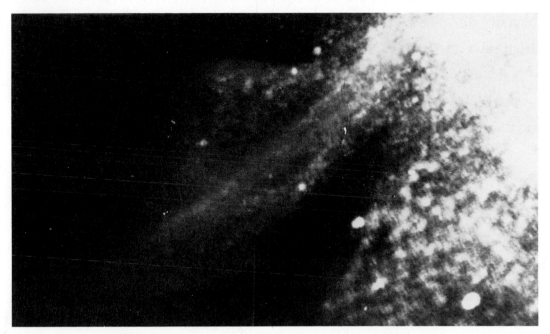

Could Nessie be a prehistoric animal like the dinosaur? These animals are believed to have died out long ago. But many people who have seen Nessie are then asked to look at pictures of prehistoric animals. They are also asked which one she looks like. Most pick the same one — the **plesiosaur** (PLEE-see-a-sore).

The plesiosaur was a giant reptile that lived millions of years ago. It had a long neck, a fat body, and a long tail. It also had small flippers like a seal.

Scientists know that plesiosaurs once lived near Loch Ness. However, plesiosaurs are believed to have died out 70 million years ago.

Some ideas about Nessie come from legends. One tells about a very big creature called the Great Orm. Drawings of it have been found on stones near Loch Ness. Some people believe this legend. They think Nessie is a huge worm.

A worm is an **invertebrate** (in-VERT-uh-bret), an animal without bones. If Nessie is a worm, that explains why none of her ancestors' bones were ever found.

However, scientists don't know of any worms that are as long or wide as Nessie is said to be.

In the sixth century, a holy man named Saint Columba came to Loch Ness. To him, Nessie was a frightening "Water monster."

The story goes like this. Saint Columba asked one of his men to swim across the lake and bring back a boat. Soon the swimmer heard a great roar. He also saw a big, wide-open mouth. The poor swimmer thought he was done for. But Saint Columba was watching. He raised his arms and cried out to the monster with holy words. And the monster was driven away.

No one can be quite sure if this story about Saint Columba and the monster really happened. But it was the first story about this monster ever written down. It was called "Of the Driving Away of a Certain Water Monster by Virtue of Prayer."

This story also raised a big question. If Saint Columba spotted Nessie in the sixth century, is she thousands of years old today? Absolutely not! Not even monsters can live that long. If Nessie is real, she must be the great-great-great-grandchild of the first one.

But how did Nessie's ancestors get into Loch Ness in the first place? Only one little river joins Loch Ness to the sea. Nessie is said to be too big to swim through this river.

Several geologists explained it this way. Thousands of years ago there was no Loch Ness. This lake was really part of the sea. The Ice Age helped change all this. Land rose between certain areas of water, making lakes.

Possibly Nessie's ancestors were trapped in Loch Ness after this happened.

For years, Nessie has puzzled scientists. Was she a mammal? A plesiosaur? Was she anything at all? Today, scientists still are not sure. Most say there is not enough information to prove she is real.

However, sometimes there are animals alive that scientists don't know about. For years, scientists were sure that a prehistoric fish called the **coelacanth** (SEE-la-kanth) was no longer alive. Then, one was found swimming in the Indian Ocean. Perhaps Nessie is like this prehistoric fish. Perhaps she is an animal long thought dead, but alive and well today.

No one will be sure what Nessie is until she is found or caught. However, looking for Nessie takes a lot of work. Loch Ness is very deep and dark. There are hardly any beaches, and in some places the water is over 900 feet (274 m) deep.

Loch Ness is also filled with rotting plant material called peat. This turns the water dark brown like coffee. Divers who look for Nessie are always disappointed. They can't see anything.

Most of the world never heard of Nessie until 1933. Then people began building a road alongside Loch Ness. Before then, hardly anyone went there. Now loads of people pass by every day. Perhaps Nessie wanted to know what all their noise was about. Whatever the reason, loads of people began seeing a monster.

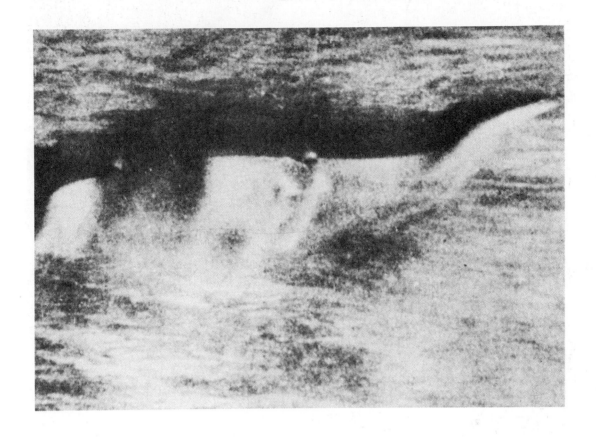

The first person to snap a picture of Nessie was a Scottish Highlander named Hugh Gray. The picture was very fuzzy, but a Scottish newspaper printed it anyway. The photograph made people very excited. Everyone wanted to know more about the monster.

Soon a big newspaperman from England came to Loch Ness. He brought along a game hunter and a photographer. Monster stories sell loads of newspapers. Shortly, the hunter found giant footprints by the shore. Everyone was very happy. Nessie had not been spotted on land before. A plaster cast was made and rushed to the British Museum.

The newspaperman was too excited to wait for the museum's answer. He ran a big story about Nessie right away. He should have waited. The museum found

something
very strange.
The footprints
had been made
by a stuffed
hippopotamus's foot.
For a while, the world
had been fooled by the hunter's trick.

Since 1934, thousands of people have reported seeing Nessie. To these people, Nessie isn't a trick. She is very real. Some people have even photographed her. None of these photographs are very clear, and they all look different.

One shows a huge body and a very long neck. It is called the Surgeon's Photograph because a doctor took it. Many believe it is Nessie's best picture. It also looks very much like a plesiosaur.

Other photographs show this:

- Three humps rising out of the lake. They are all the same size.

- Two humps. One is bigger than the other.

- One hump.

- No humps. Just a V-shaped wake.

Could any of these be Nessie? Today, scientists still are not sure.

In time, so many people became interested in Nessie that in 1962 the Loch Ness Phenomena Investigation Bureau was formed, headed by a member of the British Parliament, David James. At first, Mr. James didn't believe in Nessie. Today people from his bureau spend many hours looking for her.

Several newspapers and universities have also joined the search. Every summer, teams of scientists travel to Loch Ness for a scientific monster hunt. These expeditions use special equipment like **sonar** (SO-nar) and underwater cameras. Sonar is a way of using electronics to discover the size, depth, and movement of an object.

Unfortunately, sonar isn't perfect. Once, scientists were sure they had found Nessie. However, their monster turned out to be a large shoal of fish.

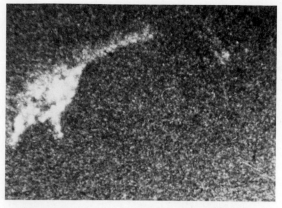

In 1976 another team of scientists took this underwater photograph. Because the waters of Loch Ness are so murky, it was difficult to get a clear photograph. Still, the scientists felt that the photograph showed the body, flippers, long neck, and head of an unknown animal. Do you think the photograph looks like the drawing of the plesiosaur below?

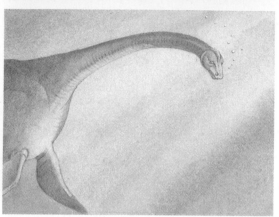

The real star of one expedition was the underwater camera. In 1975, a member of the Boston Academy of Applied Sciences took two photographs with it that could have been Nessie. One looked like a dragon's head with horns. The other looked like the body of a plesiosaur. Which one was Nessie? Both or neither? Again, the photographs were not clear enough for scientists to be sure. However, the British naturalist, Sir Peter Scott, was so sure the pictures were genuine that he gave Nessie a scientific Latin name: *Nessitara rhombopteryx.*

Today, thousands of people go to Loch Ness. Some spend hours staring at the lake through their hotel windows. Others stand all day by its shore. And still others ride around in small boats. All these people want one thing: to see the world's most famous monster — NESSIE.

I was sitting by the lake when all of a sudden...

Imagine you are on vacation in Scotland. You are visiting the famous Loch Ness. Suddenly . . .

Based on what you now know about the Loch Ness monster, write a story about spotting Nessie. You may also want to draw a picture of Nessie.

AUTHORS

Judy Donnelly

Judy Donnelly, author of *The* Titanic: *Lost . . . and Found,* remembers reading *Treasure Island* "when I was about eight years old and scouring my neighborhood in Connecticut for treasure — with no luck whatsoever." Although Donnelly never discovered a treasure, many of her books, like *Tut's Mummy Lost — and Found* and *True-Life Treasure Hunts,* open our eyes to real adventures.

Aliki

Aliki writes about fossils, both living and dead, and about a hundred other exciting subjects. She loves "writing complicated facts as clearly as possible." That way, she says, "Readers and I, who know nothing about a subject, learn a great deal by the time we are finished." Another of her many wonderful books that you might enjoy is *Mummies Made in Egypt,* which describes mummies buried long ago.

Ellen Rabinowich

Ellen Rabinowich has written for readers of all ages, but she likes writing for young people best. She has written several books for them including ones about koalas, horses, and kangaroos.

DIVE INTO THESE BOOKS

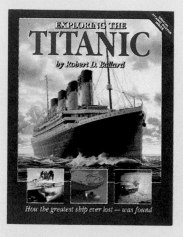

Sunken Treasure
by Gail Gibbons
On the bottom of the sea lie the treasures of many a sunken ship. Here's how treasure hunters bring up riches from these wrecks of long ago.

Mystery Monsters of Loch Ness
by Patricia Lauber
What creatures live in the dark waters of the most famous lake in Scotland? Could Nessie, the famous monster, be one of those animals?

Exploring the Titanic
by Robert D. Ballard
The exciting story and pictures tell about the discovery of the *Titanic*. Robert Ballard, the man who led the exploration, gives the story firsthand.

Treasures in the Sea

by Robert M. McClung

Treasures that lie at the bottom of the deep aren't always gold and gems. This book shows the wonder and beauty of animal life under water.

Danger — Icebergs!

by Roma Gans

Those mountains of ice called icebergs hold great danger for ships at sea. Read about giant icebergs like the one that sank the great *Titanic*.

Yeh-Shen

retold by Ai-Ling Louie
illustrated by
Ed Young

In the dim past, even before the Ch'in and the Han dynasties, there lived a cave chief of southern China by the name of Wu. As was the custom in those days, Chief Wu had taken two wives. Each wife in her turn had presented Wu with a baby daughter. But one of the wives sickened and died, and not too many days after that Chief Wu took to his bed and died too.

Yeh-Shen, the little orphan, grew to girlhood in her stepmother's home. She was a bright child and lovely too, with skin as smooth as ivory and dark pools for eyes. Her stepmother was jealous of all this beauty and goodness, for her own daughter was not pretty at all. So in her displeasure, she gave poor Yeh-Shen the heaviest and most unpleasant chores.

The only friend that Yeh-Shen had to her name was a fish she had caught and raised. It was a beautiful fish with golden eyes, and every day it would come out of the water and rest its head on the bank of the pond, waiting for Yeh-Shen to feed it. Stepmother gave Yeh-Shen little enough food for herself, but the orphan child always found

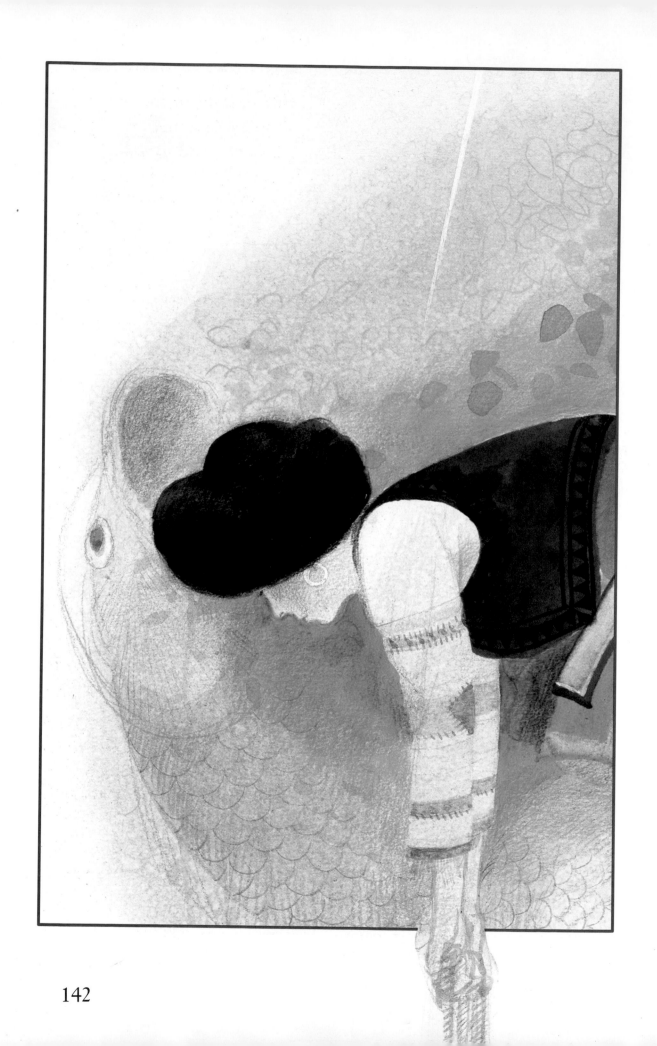

something to share with her fish, which grew to enormous size.

Somehow the stepmother heard of this. She was terribly angry to discover that Yeh-Shen had kept a secret from her. She hurried down to the pond, but she was unable to see the fish, for Yeh-Shen's pet wisely hid itself. The stepmother, however, was a crafty woman, and she soon thought of a plan. She walked home and called out, "Yeh-Shen, go and collect some firewood. But wait! The neighbors might see you. Leave your filthy coat here!" The minute the girl was out of sight, her stepmother slipped on the coat herself and went down again to the pond. This time the big fish saw Yeh-Shen's familiar jacket and heaved itself onto the bank, expecting to be fed. But the stepmother, having hidden a dagger in her sleeve, stabbed the fish, wrapped it in her garments, and took it home to cook for dinner.

When Yeh-Shen came to the pond that evening, she found her pet had disappeared. Overcome with grief, the girl collapsed on the ground and dropped her tears into the still waters of the pond.

"Ah, poor child!" a voice said.

Yeh-Shen sat up to find a very old man looking down at her. He wore the coarsest of clothes, and his hair flowed down over his shoulders.

"Kind uncle, who may you be?" Yeh-Shen asked.

"That is not important, my child. All you must know is that I have been sent to tell you of the wondrous powers of your fish."

"My fish, but sir . . ." The girl's eyes filled with

tears, and she could not go on.

The old man sighed and said, "Yes, my child, your fish is no longer alive, and I must tell you that your stepmother is once more the cause of your sorrow." Yeh-Shen gasped in horror, but the old man went on. "Let us not dwell on things that are past," he said, "for I have come bringing you a gift. Now you must listen carefully to this: The bones of your fish are filled with a powerful spirit. Whenever you are in serious need, you must kneel before them and let them know your heart's desire. But do not waste their gifts."

Yeh-Shen wanted to ask the old sage many more questions, but he rose to the sky before she could utter another word. With heavy heart, Yeh-Shen made her way to the dung heap to gather the remains of her friend.

Time went by, and Yeh-Shen, who was often left alone, took comfort in speaking to the bones of her fish.

When she was hungry, which happened quite often, Yeh-Shen asked the bones for food. In this way, Yeh-Shen managed to live from day to day, but she lived in dread that her stepmother would discover her secret and take even that away from her.

So the time passed and spring came. Festival time was approaching: It was the busiest time of the year. Such cooking and cleaning and sewing there was to be done! Yeh-Shen had hardly a moment's rest. At the spring festival young men and young women from the village hoped to meet and to choose whom they would marry. How Yeh-Shen longed to go! But her stepmother had other plans. She hoped to find a husband for her own daughter and did not want any man to see the beauteous Yeh-Shen first.

When finally the holiday arrived, the stepmother and her daughter dressed themselves in their finery and filled their baskets with sweetmeats. "You must remain at home now, and watch to see that no one steals fruit from our trees," her stepmother told Yeh-Shen, and then she departed for the banquet with her own daughter.

As soon as she was alone, Yeh-Shen went to speak to the bones of her fish. "Oh, dear friend,"

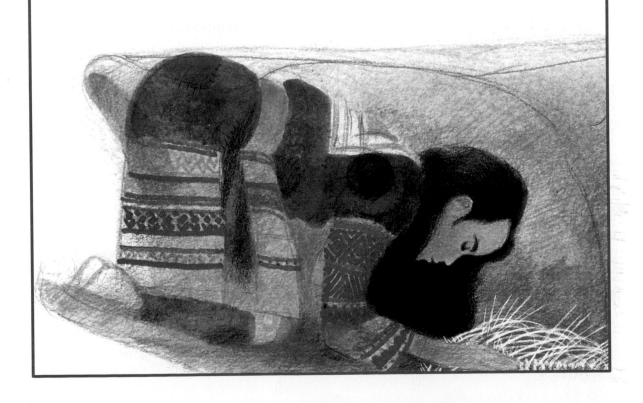

she said, kneeling before the precious bones, "I long to go to the festival, but I cannot show myself in these rags. Is there somewhere I could borrow clothes fit to wear to the feast?" At once she found herself dressed in a gown of azure blue, with a cloak of kingfisher feathers draped around her shoulders. Best of all, on her tiny feet were the most beautiful slippers she had ever seen. They were woven of golden threads, in a pattern like the scales of a fish, and the glistening soles were made of solid gold. There was magic in the shoes, for they should have been quite heavy,

yet when Yeh-Shen walked, her feet felt as light as air.

"Be sure you do not lose your golden shoes," said the spirit of the bones. Yeh-Shen promised to be careful. Delighted with her transformation, she bid a fond farewell to the bones of her fish as she slipped off to join in the merrymaking.

That day Yeh-Shen turned many a head as she appeared at the feast. All around her people whispered, "Look at that beautiful girl! Who can she be?"

But above this, Stepsister was heard to say, "Mother, does she not resemble our Yeh-Shen?"

Upon hearing this, Yeh-Shen jumped up and ran off before her stepsister could look closely at her. She raced down the mountainside, and in doing so, she lost one of her golden slippers. No sooner had the shoe

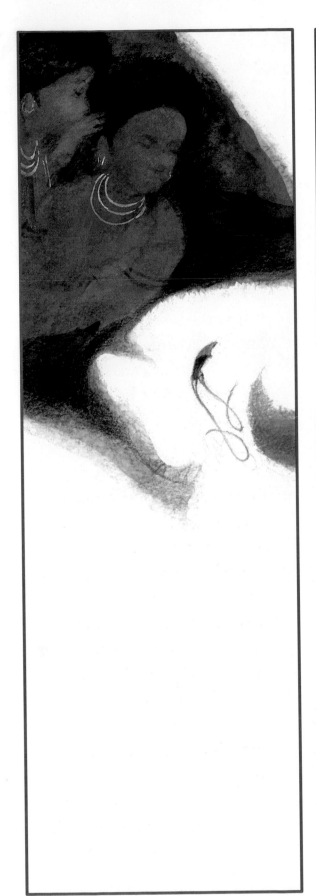

fallen from her foot than all her fine clothes turned back to rags. Only one thing remained — a tiny golden shoe. Yeh-Shen hurried to the bones of her fish and returned the slipper, promising to find its mate. But now the bones were silent. Sadly Yeh-Shen realized that she had lost her only friend. She hid the little shoe in her bedstraw, and went outside to cry. Leaning against a fruit tree, she sobbed and sobbed until she fell asleep.

The stepmother left the gathering to check on Yeh-Shen, but when she returned home she found the girl sound asleep, with her arms wrapped around a fruit tree. So thinking no more of her, the stepmother rejoined the party. Meantime, a villager had found the shoe. Recognizing its worth, he sold it to a merchant,

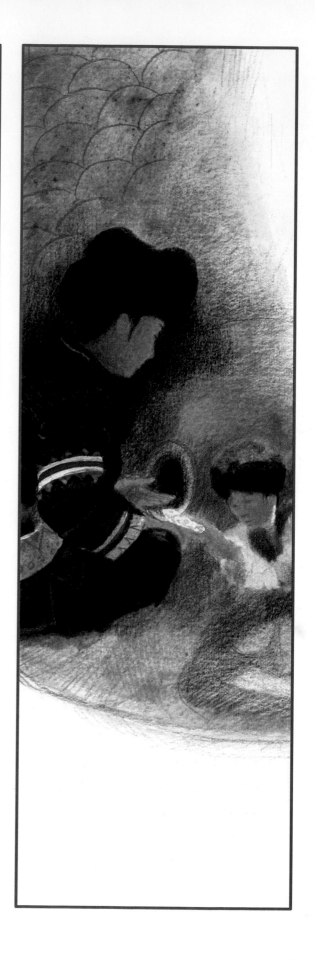

who presented it in turn to the king of the island kingdom of T'o Han.

The king was more than happy to accept the slipper as a gift. He was entranced by the tiny thing, which was shaped of the most precious of metals, yet which made no sound when touched to stone. The more he marveled at its beauty, the more determined he became to find the woman to whom the shoe belonged.

A search was begun among the ladies of his own kingdom, but all who tried on the sandal found it impossibly small. Undaunted, the king ordered the search widened to include the cave women from the countryside where the slipper had been found. Since he realized it would take many years for every woman to come to his island and test her foot in the slipper, the king thought of a way to get the right woman to come forward. He ordered the sandal placed in a pavilion by the side of the road near where it had been found, and his herald announced that the shoe was to be returned to its original owner. Then from a nearby hiding place, the king and his men settled down to watch and wait for a woman with tiny feet to come and claim her slipper.

All that day the pavilion was crowded with cave women who had come to test a foot in the shoe. Yeh-Shen's stepmother and stepsister were among them, but not Yeh-Shen — they had told her to stay home. By day's end, although many women had eagerly tried to put on the slipper, it still had not been worn. Wearily, the king continued his vigil into the night.

It wasn't until the blackest part of night, while the moon hid behind a cloud, that Yeh-Shen dared to show her face at the pavilion, and even then she tiptoed timidly across the wide floor. Sinking down to her knees, the girl in rags examined the tiny shoe. Only when she was sure that this was the missing mate to her own golden slipper did she dare pick it up. At last she could return both little shoes to the fish bones. Surely then her beloved spirit would speak to her again.

Now the king's first thought, on seeing

Yeh-Shen take the precious slipper, was to throw the girl into prison as a thief. But when she turned to leave, he caught a glimpse of her face. At once the king was struck by the sweet harmony of her features, which seemed so out of keeping with the rags she wore. It was then that he took a closer look and noticed that she walked upon the tiniest feet he had ever seen.

With a wave of his hand, the king signaled that this tattered creature was to be allowed to depart with the golden slipper. Quietly, the king's men slipped off and followed her home.

All this time, Yeh-Shen was unaware of the excitement she had caused. She had made her way home and was about to hide both sandals in her bedding when there was a pounding at the door. Yeh-Shen went to see who

it was — and found a king at her doorstep. She was very frightened at first, but the king spoke to her in a kind voice and asked her to try the golden slippers on her feet. The maiden did as she was told, and as she stood in her golden shoes, her rags were transformed once more into the feathered cloak and beautiful azure gown.

Her loveliness made her seem a heavenly being, and the king suddenly knew in his heart that he had found his true love.

Not long after this, Yeh-Shen was married to the king. But fate was not so gentle with her stepmother and stepsister. Since they had been unkind to his beloved, the king would not permit Yeh-Shen to bring them to his palace. They remained in their cave home, where one day, it is said, they were crushed to death in a shower of flying stones.

At midnight Pío was sleepy, but each time he started to nod off and lie down, the sharp pricking of the *cadillos* woke him up. Slowly the hours ticked by.

Then to the east Pío saw the rosy glow of dawn. The next moment he heard faintly — very faintly — the sound of a gallop.

Between him and the rising sun he made out the shape of a horse. Instantly Pío leaped to his feet and sped toward the trees where the horse had disappeared. As he crashed through the underbrush he saw a flash of color, then another, and another. It was a little horse, gleaming with the seven colors of the rainbow in the soft dawn light.

Slowly Pío approached. He was just about to grab the little horse about the neck when the horse said, "Do not touch me. If you let me go, I will never trample your maize field again."

Pío stopped. He looked at the little horse. "Why should I let you go?" he asked gently.

"Because if you do, I will grant you three favors for your kindness."

"What kind of favors?" Pío asked.

"Whenever you find yourself in danger or want something very much but cannot get it, all you have to say is:

Aquí de mi caballito — Come here, my little horse' — and I will come at once to help you."

Pío thought a moment, then nodded his head. "All right," he said.

"Thank you," said the little horse and disappeared in a puff of rainbow-colored smoke.

Pío rushed home to tell his father that the maize field would never be trampled again. Pío's father was overjoyed with the news. But the two brothers were jealous because Pío had outwitted them and with every day that passed, their jealousy grew and grew.

Not long afterwards Tano died, and the two older brothers took over the house. Now Pío had to wait on them hand and foot. They sent him to the kitchen to cook. They sent him to the stables to clean. They sent him to tend the maize. He ran from kitchen to field to stables, upstairs and downstairs, doing all the work while his brothers ate, drank, slept, and rode to town on their horses.

One day, Carlos and Pedro galloped up to the house after spending the morning in town. They seemed unusually excited. As Pío served their lunch he learned why. The great and wealthy Don Nicanor had decided it was time for his daughter to marry. But Don Nicanor was a strange man. And Leonor's husband was to be chosen in a strange way. That was all Pío's brothers could talk about as they ate their lunch.

"I know I can pass Don Nicanor's tests," boasted Carlos.

"What are the tests?" asked Pío who was serving the soup.

"That doesn't concern you," said Carlos, "and my soup is cold."

"So is mine," said Pedro. "Go heat it up!"

While he was in the kitchen pretending to warm the soup — which was not really cold at all — Pío listened to his brothers. The man who could ride his horse at full gallop past Leonor's balcony and toss a rubber ball into her lap three days in a row would win Leonor's hand in marriage.

Carlos and Pedro decided to try their luck at once. They put on their Sunday suits and rode off. As soon as they were out of sight, Pío went to the patio and called: "*Aquí de mi caballito* — Come here, my little horse." In an instant there appeared a puff of rainbow-colored smoke and out stepped the little horse.

"What do you want, Pío?"

"I want to marry Leonor, Don Nicanor's beautiful daughter. But to do so, I must ride at full gallop past her balcony three times and each time I must toss a little rubber ball into her lap. Can you help me?"

"I can and I will, but only if you make me a promise."

"What sort of promise?" asked Pío.

"You must promise not to ask questions — not one question — no matter what I do."

"I promise," said Pío.

160

And suddenly Pío found himself richly dressed, seated on the little horse's back, holding a rubber ball in his hand.

Swift as the wind they galloped and reached the town just as Carlos and Pedro started to ride past Leonor's balcony. Carlos rode first, but when he tossed his rubber ball, his strong arm threw it so hard that it bounced off the wall above Leonor's head.

"Ah ha!" said clever Pedro to himself, "I shall not throw my ball so hard." As he sped by he tossed his ball, but he did not toss it hard enough and it bounced at Leonor's feet and rolled off the balcony.

Suddenly a huge shout arose from the crowd for, galloping toward the balcony at lightning speed, came the rainbow-colored horse with a richly dressed rider in the saddle. As they sped past the balcony the rider tossed the ball very gently into Leonor's lap.

The crowd cheered. Don Nicanor leaped to his feet to welcome the mysterious rider, but the rainbow-colored horse did not stop. It kept on running until it reached Pío's house. Pío wanted very much to ask the little horse why he had galloped straight home in such a hurry, but he remembered his promise and kept silent.

"Step down, Pío," said the little horse and before Pío's feet touched the ground, it disappeared in a puff of rainbow-colored smoke. Pío was once again dressed in his working clothes.

By and by he heard his brothers ride into the yard. They strode into the house, slamming the door behind them.

"Supper!" yelled Carlos.

"Supper!" shouted Pedro.

Pío hurried to the kitchen, but he could still hear his brothers talking in angry voices.

"That stranger is robbing us of our chance," growled Carlos.

"I wonder if we know him," said Pedro.

In the kitchen Pío softly chanted:

Maybe no,

Maybe yes,

Who he is you'll have to guess.

"Stop that silly chanting and bring in the soup!" shouted Carlos.

"And it better be hot this time!" yelled Pedro.

The following morning the two brothers rode off to try their luck once more. No sooner had they swung into their saddles when Pío went out to the patio and called: "*Aquí de mi caballito* — Come here, my little horse." Once again, out of a puff of rainbow-colored smoke, stepped the little horse. Pío said what he wanted and the little horse answered, "Today you must go dressed more richly than yesterday." And again, Pío stood magnificently dressed, holding a rubber ball in his hand.

"Climb up," said the little horse, and off they went, faster than the wind itself.

The town was overflowing with people who had heard about the rainbow-colored horse and the mysterious rider. At one end of the street young men on horseback were lined up awaiting their turns to ride past the balcony. One by one they galloped headlong down the street throwing rubber balls every which way except into Leonor's lap. Carlos and Pedro were way back near the end of the line. When their turns came, Carlos galloped off first. Remembering his mistake of the day before he threw the ball very weakly — too weakly. It landed at Leonor's feet and rolled off the balcony. Then Pedro, remembering his poor throw, gave the ball a hard toss as he galloped past. But it hit the wall above Leonor's head and bounced into the crowd.

Suddenly, out of nowhere, the rainbow-colored horse and the mysterious rider appeared. Like a flash they sped past the balcony. Once again Pío tossed the ball gently into Leonor's lap. The crowd roared its approval and Don Nicanor raised his arms to halt the rider but the little horse never stopped till it reached Pío's house.

"Step down, Pío," it said, and before Pío could even say thank you, it had disappeared in a cloud of rainbow-colored smoke. Once again in his working clothes, Pío shook his head. Why was the little horse running away from town in such a hurry? If only he had not promised not to ask even one question. But a promise is a promise, he told himself. And he went into the house.

After a while Pedro and Carlos came riding into the yard. The dark looks on their faces showed their anger.

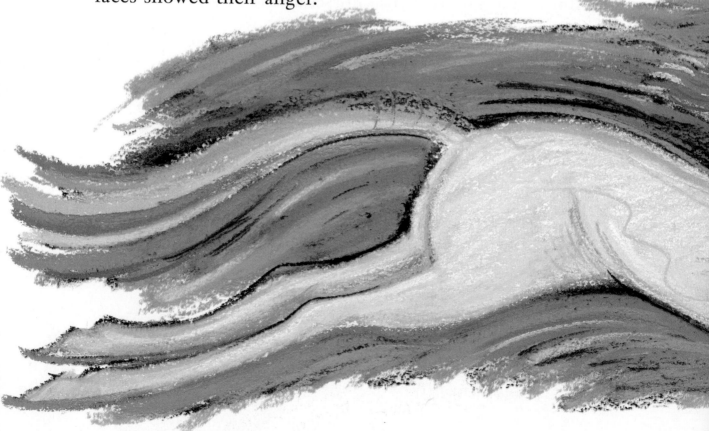

"I would have succeeded if my saddle hadn't slipped," growled Carlos.

"I would have done it if my stirrup had held," snarled Pedro.

"Why does that stranger keep coming then riding away? I wonder who he is," said Carlos.

"Do you think he is someone we know?" asked Pedro.

Inside the house, Pío was listening, and he chanted once again:

> Maybe no,
> Maybe yes,
> Who he is you'll have to guess.

"Stop that silly nonsense," snapped Carlos.

"Why isn't dinner ready? What do you do all day long?" demanded Pedro.

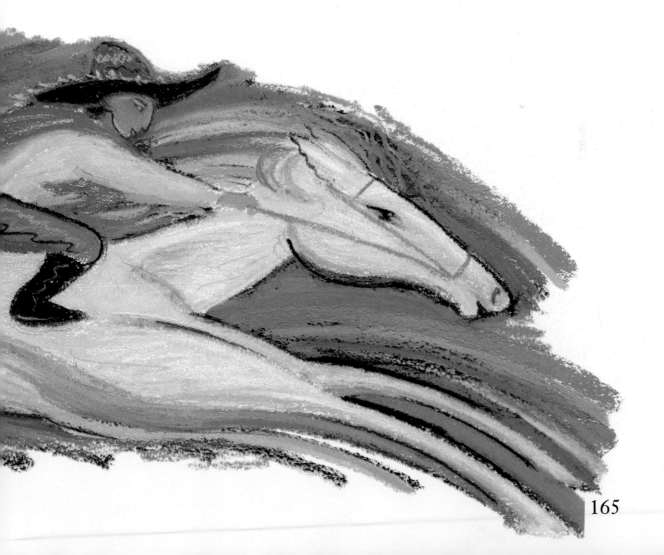

The following day the two brothers went off again. Pío watched them until they were out of sight. Then he went to the patio and called: "*Aquí de mi caballito* — Come here, my little horse."

The little horse appeared at once. Pío told it what he wanted.

"Today you shall go dressed as you are," said the little horse. "Climb up. We must be off."

If the little horse had run fast the first day and faster the second, today it almost flew. It flew so fast that all anyone could see was a blur of color. As it passed Leonor's balcony Pío tossed the ball very gently into Leonor's lap. Then he grabbed the reins for the ride home. But the little horse did not run away this time. It circled back to the spot where Don Nicanor stood waiting.

Cries of *Bravo!* and *Olé!* filled the air. People threw their hats into the air. But Pío paid no attention. He was listening to the little horse.

"Pío, now we must part. Because I was an enchanted horse, because I helped you three times, but most of all because you kept your promise, the spell that was put upon me has been broken. I am free to return to the place I came from. Thank you. Go now to the balcony and claim your prize."

As the little horse spoke, a rainbow-colored mist swirled about them and when it lifted, the little horse had vanished. A moment later a beautiful rainbow spread across the sky and Pío found himself between his two brothers. They could not believe their eyes.

"Pío, are you, our own brother, the strange rider?" both asked in one voice.

167

Before they could ask more, Pío had climbed up to the balcony to claim Leonor's hand in marriage. Only then did Carlos and Pedro remember the little chant:

Maybe no,

Maybe yes,

Who he is you'll have to guess.

They felt very sorry about the way they had treated their brother. Bowing their heads in shame, they turned their horses toward home.

But when Pío noticed his brothers leaving, he called them back. Then and there he forgave them and invited them to the wedding.

"Bring the *cuatro*," Pío told them. "There must be happy music."

And they did. Carlos sang and Pedro played the *cuatro*, then Pedro sang and Carlos played the *cuatro*. It was the best and merriest wedding the town had ever seen. Everyone agreed that there was only one thing more beautiful than the music — the smiles on the faces of Pío and Leonor.

MAY THE BEST MAN WIN!

Pío was quiet and gentle, but he was also very clever. Remember, it was Pío who thought of putting the *cadillos* on the hammock to keep himself awake.

Suppose Pío had not had the rainbow-colored horse to help him. What clever idea might he have thought of to win the contest?

Write a paragraph that tells what you think he might have done.

Pura Belpré

Pura Belpré was born in Puerto Rico into a family of storytellers. Throughout her life, she enjoyed putting on puppet shows and telling stories based on the legends of her native land.

When she grew up, Pura Belpré moved to New York and became a children's librarian. In the library she looked for the folktales she had heard at home in Puerto Rico. When she could not find any, she decided to write her own. She has written books of these folktales, as well as other kinds of stories. *Santiago, Once in Puerto Rico,* and *Dance of the Animals* are three of Pura Belpré's popular books for children.

The Art of
Fairy Tales

1.

Fairy tales have been told over and over again in many different ways, by many different writers and storytellers. They have also been illustrated by many different artists.

Here are some illustrations from well-known fairy tales. How many do you recognize?

2.

3.

4.

5.

Mufaro's Beautiful Daughters

written and illustrated
by John Steptoe

A LONG TIME AGO, in a certain place in Africa, a small
village lay across a river and half a day's journey from a
city where a great king lived. A man named Mufaro lived
in this village with his two daughters, who were called

173

Manyara and Nyasha. Everyone agreed that Manyara and Nyasha were very beautiful.

Manyara was almost always in a bad temper. She teased her sister whenever their father's back was turned, and she had been heard to say, "Someday, Nyasha, I will be a queen, and you will be a servant in my household."

"If that should come to pass," Nyasha responded, "I will be pleased to serve you. But why do you say such things? You are clever and strong and beautiful. Why are you so unhappy?"

"Because everyone talks about how kind *you* are, and they praise everything you do," Manyara replied. "I'm certain that Father loves you best. But when I am a queen, everyone will know that your silly kindness is only weakness."

Nyasha was sad that Manyara felt this way, but she ignored her sister's words and went about her chores. Nyasha kept a small plot of land, on which she grew millet, sunflowers, yams, and vegetables. She always sang as she worked, and some said it was her singing that made her crops more bountiful than anyone else's.

One day, Nyasha noticed a small garden snake resting beneath a yam vine. "Good day, little Nyoka," she called to him. "You are welcome here. You will keep away any creatures who might spoil my vegetables." She bent forward, gave the little snake a loving pat on the head, and then returned to her work.

From that day on, Nyoka was always at Nyasha's side when she tended her garden. It was said that she sang all the more sweetly when he was there.

Mufaro knew nothing of how Manyara treated Nyasha. Nyasha was too considerate of her father's feelings to complain, and Manyara was always careful to behave herself when Mufaro was around.

Early one morning, a messenger from the city arrived. The Great King wanted a wife. "The Most Worthy and Beautiful Daughters in the Land are invited to appear before the King, and he will choose one to become Queen!" the messenger proclaimed.

Mufaro called Manyara and Nyasha to him. "It would be a great honor to have one of you chosen," he said. "Prepare yourselves to journey to the city. I will call together all our friends to make a wedding party. We will leave tomorrow as the sun rises."

"But, my father," Manyara said sweetly, "it would be painful for either of us to leave you, even to be wife to the king. I know Nyasha would grieve to death if she were parted from you. I am strong. Send me to the city, and let poor Nyasha be happy here with you."

Mufaro beamed with pride. "The king has asked for the most worthy and the most beautiful. No, Manyara, I cannot send you alone. Only a king can choose between two such worthy daughters. Both of you must go!"

That night, when everyone was asleep, Manyara stole quietly out of the village. She had never been in the forest at night before, and she was frightened, but her greed to be the first to appear before the king drove her on. In her hurry, she almost stumbled over a small boy who suddenly appeared, standing in the path.

"Please," said the boy. "I am hungry. Will you give me something to eat?"

"I have brought only enough for myself," Manyara replied.

"But, please!" said the boy.

"I am so *very* hungry."

"Out of my way, boy! Tomorrow I will become your queen. How dare you stand in my path?"

After traveling for what seemed to be a great distance, Manyara came to a small clearing. There, silhouetted against the moonlight, was an old woman seated on a large stone.

The old woman spoke. "I will give you some advice, Manyara. Soon after you pass the place where two paths cross, you will see a grove of trees. They will laugh at you. You must not laugh in return. Later, you will meet a man with his head under his arm. You must be polite to him."

"How do you know my name? How dare you advise your future queen? Stand aside, you ugly old woman!"

Manyara scolded, and then rushed on her way
without looking back.

Just as the old woman had foretold,
Manyara came to a grove of trees, and they did
indeed seem to be laughing at her.

"I must be calm," Manyara thought. "I will
not be frightened." She looked up at the trees
and laughed out loud. "I laugh at you, trees!"
she shouted, and she hurried on.

It was not yet dawn when Manyara heard the
sound of rushing water. "The river must be up
ahead," she thought. "The great city is just on
the other side."

But there, on the rise, she saw a man with his
head tucked under his arm. Manyara ran past
him without speaking. "A queen acknowledges

only those who please her," she said to herself.
"I will be queen. I will be queen," she chanted,
as she hurried on toward the city.

Nyasha woke at the first light of dawn. As
she put on her finest garments, she thought how
her life might be changed forever beyond this day.
"I'd much prefer to live here," she admitted to
herself. "I'd hate to leave this village and never
see my father or sing to little Nyoka again."

Her thoughts were interrupted by loud
shouts and a commotion from the wedding
party assembled outside. Manyara was missing!
Everyone bustled about, searching and calling
for her. When they found her footprints on
the path that led to the city, they decided to go
on as planned.

As the wedding party moved through the forest, brightly plumed birds darted about in the cool green shadows beneath the trees. Though anxious about her sister, Nyasha was soon filled with excitement about all there was to see.

They were deep in the forest when she saw the small boy standing by the side of the path.

"You must be hungry," she said, and handed him a yam she had brought for her lunch. The boy smiled and disappeared as quietly as he had come.

Later, as they were approaching the place where the two paths crossed, the old woman appeared and silently pointed the way to the city. Nyasha thanked her and gave her a small pouch filled with sunflower seeds.

The sun was high in the sky when the party came to the grove of towering trees. Their uppermost branches seemed to bow down to Nyasha as she passed beneath them.

At last, someone announced that they were near their destination.

Nyasha ran ahead and topped the rise before the others could catch up with her. She stood transfixed at her first sight of the city. "Oh, my father," she called. "A great spirit must stand guard here! Just look at what lies before us. I never in all my life dreamed there could be anything so beautiful!"

Arm in arm, Nyasha and her father descended the hill, crossed the river, and approached the city gate. Just as they entered through the great doors, the air was rent by piercing cries, and Manyara ran wildly out of a chamber at the center of the enclosure. When she saw Nyasha, she fell upon her, sobbing.

"Do not go to the king, my sister. Oh, please, Father, do not let her go!" she cried hysterically. "There's a great monster there, a snake with five heads! He said that he knew all my faults and that I displeased him. He would have swallowed me alive if I had not run. Oh, my sister, please do not go inside that place."

It frightened Nyasha to see her sister so upset. But, leaving her father to comfort Manyara, she bravely made her way to the chamber and opened the door.

On the seat of the great chief's stool lay the little garden snake. Nyasha laughed with relief and joy.

"My little friend!" she exclaimed. "It's such a pleasure to see you, but why are you here?"

"I am the king," Nyoka replied.

And there, before Nyasha's eyes, the garden snake changed shape.

"I am the king. I am also the hungry boy

with whom you shared a yam in the forest and the old woman to whom you made a gift of sunflower seeds. But you know me best as Nyoka. Because I have been all of these, I know you to be the Most Worthy and Most Beautiful Daughter in the Land. It would make me very happy if you would be my wife."

And so it was that, a long time ago, Nyasha agreed to be married. The king's mother and sisters took Nyasha to their house, and the wedding preparations began. The best weavers in the land laid out their finest cloth for her wedding garments. Villagers from all around were invited to the celebration, and a great feast was held. Nyasha prepared the bread for the wedding feast from millet that had been brought from her village.

Mufaro proclaimed to all who would hear him that he was the happiest father in all the land, for he was blessed with two beautiful and worthy daughters — Nyasha, the queen; and Manyara, a servant in the queen's household.

Suppose that *Mufaro's Beautiful Daughters* took place in the present, in your own town or city. Work with a friend to rewrite the story as a modern fairy tale. Make sure that a reader would know *where* and *when* your story takes place!

John Steptoe

John Steptoe grew up in the Bedford-Stuyvesant section of New York City. This was also the setting of his first book, *Stevie*, which he wrote when he was seventeen.

John Steptoe was both a writer and an illustrator. It took him two years to illustrate *Mufaro's Beautiful Daughters*.

Another book by John Steptoe that you might enjoy reading is *The Story of Jumping Mouse*, a Native American legend about an unselfish mouse.

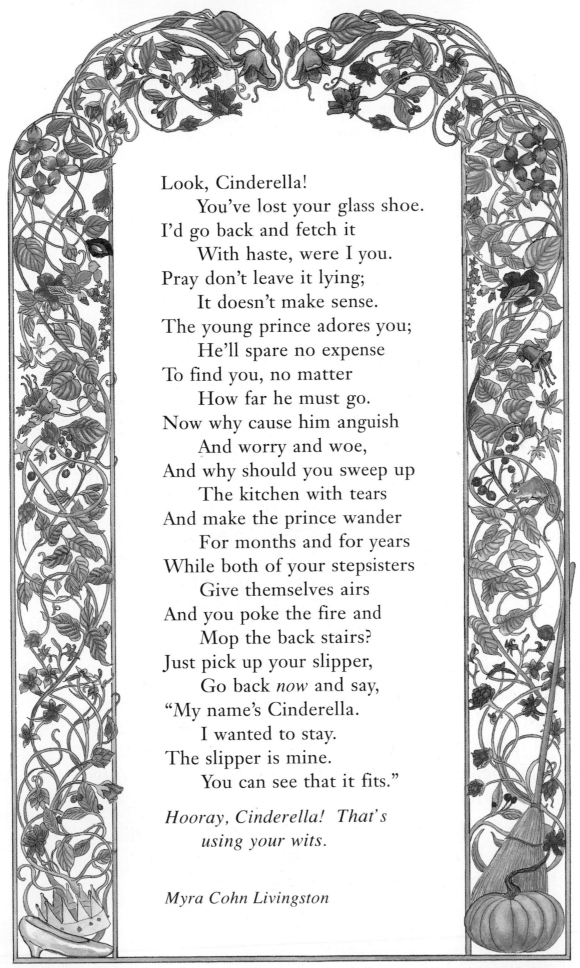

Look, Cinderella!
> You've lost your glass shoe.
I'd go back and fetch it
> With haste, were I you.
Pray don't leave it lying;
> It doesn't make sense.
The young prince adores you;
> He'll spare no expense
To find you, no matter
> How far he must go.
Now why cause him anguish
> And worry and woe,
And why should you sweep up
> The kitchen with tears
And make the prince wander
> For months and for years
While both of your stepsisters
> Give themselves airs
And you poke the fire and
> Mop the back stairs?
Just pick up your slipper,
> Go back *now* and say,
"My name's Cinderella.
> I wanted to stay.
The slipper is mine.
> You can see that it fits."

Hooray, Cinderella! That's
> *using your wits.*

Myra Cohn Livingston

187

Not every Cinderella story ends happily ever after. Here's a topsy-turvy version of "Cinderella" that was written by an eleven-year-old student.

Cinderella

Once there lived a widow who had a daughter called Cinderella. She was the ugliest girl in town. She had two stepsisters called Mary and Sue. They had very beautiful long hair and cute faces. Cinderella was jealous of their beauty. She made them work. While other girls had fun, they stayed home and worked: cooking, washing, scrubbing, and the lowest jobs.

As time went by, the stepsisters grew very sad. One day, a letter came from Zack inviting Mary and Sue to his party.

Cinderella was furious at not being invited and told Zack that if she could not go, she would tell people how cruel he was to his dog. Zack quickly agreed. Cinderella was so happy. She got out her outfit for the next night. Mary could not find anything to wear. So, when Cinderella left in her sports car, Mary and Sue went out to shop for clothes. The night was cold. There was a full moon and twigs were crackling. Suddenly one of the shadows moved.

On an impulse, Sue got a stick and walked to the shadow. It was Zack. They were relieved and happy about the joke. They took Zack's car. The party was in full blast when they arrived. Cinderella was there. Everyone danced, chatted, and laughed. It was fun. But, suddenly, Cinderella's mom came in with a broom. She was furious. Cinderella had forgotten to lock the door and everything was stolen. She chased Cinderella until they got lost. Then a fairy came. She touched everyone lightly and they were changed to small fairies, and now, whenever there is a full moon, you can hear laughter. You can also hear the howl of Cinderella.

Ann-Marie Ekstrom
Hong Kong International School
Repulse Bay, Hong Kong, 1987

The Culture of Ghana

Traditional Ways in Ghana

READING FOCUS

Traditional and modern ways of life exist side by side in Ghana. What are some traditional ways? What are some modern ways?

Key Terms

- compound
- pods

Africa is a continent with many different kinds of land forms. Some African countries are in mountains. Others are in deserts. Still others are in low-lying rain forests.

Ghana is a country in West Africa. A great deal of Ghana is covered with thick forests. Look at the map of Ghana below.

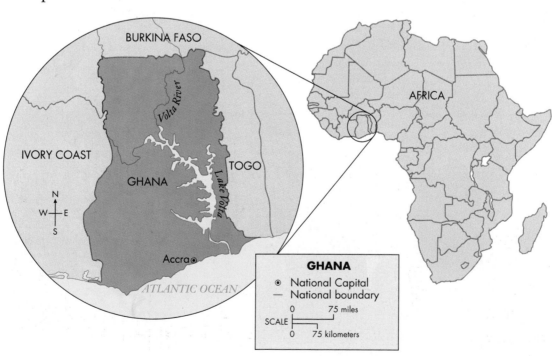

BURKINA FASO

Volta River

IVORY COAST

TOGO

GHANA

Lake Volta

N
W   E
S

Accra

ATLANTIC OCEAN

AFRICA

GHANA

⊙ National Capital
— National boundary

0   75 miles
SCALE
0   75 kilometers

Village Life in Ghana

Most people in Ghana are farmers. They live in small towns or villages and work in nearby fields. Roads are cut through the forests so that farmers can walk easily from their villages to their fields. In many villages, people live in houses that are built around courtyards. A house and courtyard together are known as a **compound**.

A family group lives in each compound. Very often the father will continue to live in the home where he grew up. The wife and children may live in the wife's mother's house. So in each compound there may be a grandmother and several mothers with their children. There may also be uncles and aunts.

Sometimes the people in a compound gather together to listen to a story. The people of Ghana are famous for their stories.

Ghana is also well known for its fine traditional crafts. Workers today still use the same methods that have been used for hundreds of years to weave cloth, carve wood, and make beautiful gold jewelry.

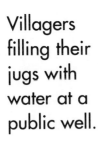
Villagers filling their jugs with water at a public well.

Differences in Ghana

There are thousands of small towns and villages in Ghana. But not all village people live the same way. The people in one village may be very different from the people in another village. They may eat different foods. They may live in different types of houses. They may wear different types of clothes. They may have different beliefs. And most important, they may speak different languages.

In Ghana, more than fifty different languages are spoken. People from one village may not be able to understand the language spoken in another village. This has always been a problem in Ghana. But today, children go to school to learn English. As a result, many Ghanaians (GAH-nee-uhnz) speak two languages. They speak one language with their friends or their family. They speak English with people from other parts of Ghana.

Children learning English at a school in eastern Ghana.

196

New Ways in Ghana

Many people in Ghana today are leaving their small towns and farms. They are moving to the cities. Accra (ah-KRAH) is Ghana's biggest city. It is also that country's capital. Some people look for work in the offices and factories of Accra. Others go to colleges or universities. They learn skills so they can get good jobs and help the Ghanaian people.

Power for the Future Until recently, most countries in Africa had very few factories. If people in Ghana wanted factory products, they had to buy them from other countries.

Ghana decided to build its own factories to make things Ghanaians wanted. But Ghana needed one important thing before it could build factories. It needed power to run machines.

One good source of power is running water. The people of Ghana knew that fast-flowing water can run machines that make

A modern public library in Accra, Ghana's capital.

electricity. So they built a huge dam across the mighty Volta River. The Akosombo (ah-koh-SOHM-boh) Dam is one of the highest dams in the world. It now controls the flow of the Volta River.

The Akosombo Dam has brought great changes to Ghana. The dam makes electricity for Ghana's cities. There is enough power to sell to the neighboring countries of Togo and Benin. The dam also makes electricity to run machines in new factories in Ghana. Today Ghana has factories that make cloth, cement, paper, cars, and chemicals. Many of Ghana's plans for the future are possible because of the great dam at Akosombo.

Chocolate for the World

While some Ghanaians have left their villages to work in the new factories, many are still farmers. Cacao (kah-KAH-oh) beans are their most important crop. Did you have cocoa or hot chocolate for breakfast this morning? If you did, it may have come from Ghana.

Cacao trees grow about seven meters (twenty-three feet) high. They have large **pods** about the size and shape of two hands cupped together. Inside each pod are cacao beans. The green pods turn red or yellow when they ripen. Then the farmer cuts the pods from the cacao tree and splits them open. The farmer puts the beans in big piles to dry and grow sweeter. Then the beans are roasted and ground into powder.

What can be made from cacao beans? By mixing together different types of beans, people make all kinds of chocolate products. They make baking chocolate, cocoa, milk chocolate, and sweet and semisweet chocolate.

Today, chocolate is popular in most of the world. Americans eat more chocolate than any other people.

Opposite Page:
Left, Cacao tree with bean pods.
Right, Cacao beans removed from their pods, drying under the hot Ghanaian sun.

CHECK UP

- What are some traditional ways of life in Ghana? What are some modern ways?

- How do most people in Ghana make a living?

- Why does Ghana have a language problem?

- Why are many people in Ghana today moving to the city?

- What is Ghana's most important crop?

Glossary

Some of the words in this book may have pronunciations or meanings you do not know. This glossary can help you by telling you how to pronounce those words and by telling you the meanings with which those words are used in this book.

You can find out the correct pronunciation of any glossary word by using the special spelling after the word and the pronunciation key that runs across the bottom of the glossary pages.

The full pronunciation key opposite shows how to pronounce each consonant and vowel in a special spelling. The pronunciation key at the bottom of the glossary pages is a shortened form of the full key.

FULL PRONUNCIATION KEY

Consonant Sounds

b	**b**i**b**	k	**c**at, **kick**, pi**que**	th	pa**th**, **th**in
ch	**ch**ur**ch**	l	**l**id, need**l**e	*th*	ba**the**, **th**is
d	**d**ee**d**	m	a**m**, **m**an, **mum**	v	ca**v**e, **v**al**v**e,
f	**f**ast, **f**i**f**e, o**ff**,	n	**n**o, sudde**n**		**v**ine
	phase, rou**gh**	ng	thi**ng**	w	**w**ith
g	**g**a**g**	p	**p**o**p**	y	**y**es
h	**h**at	r	**r**oa**r**	z	ro**s**e, **s**i**z**e,
hw	**wh**ich	s	mi**ss**, **s**au**c**e, **s**ee		**x**ylophone,
j	**j**u**dg**e	sh	di**sh**, **sh**ip		**z**ebra
		t	**t**igh**t**	zh	gara**g**e,
					plea**s**ure, vi**s**ion

Vowel Sounds

ă	p**a**t	î	d**ea**r, d**ee**r,	ou	c**ow**, **ou**t
ā	**ai**d, th**èy**, p**ay**		f**ie**rce, m**e**re	ŭ	c**u**t, r**ou**gh
â	**ai**r, c**a**re, w**ea**r	ŏ	p**o**t, h**o**rrible	û	f**i**rm, h**ea**rd,
ä	f**a**ther	ō	g**o**, r**ow**, t**oe**		t**e**rm, t**u**rn,
ĕ	p**e**t, pl**e**asure	ô	**a**lter, c**au**ght,		w**o**rd
ē	b**e**, b**ee**, **ea**sy,		f**o**r, p**aw**	yo͞o	ab**u**se, **u**se
	s**ei**ze	oi	b**oy**, n**oi**se, **oi**l	ə	**a**bout, sil**e**nt,
ĭ	p**i**t	o͝o	b**oo**k		penc**i**l, lem**o**n,
ī	b**y**, g**uy**, p**ie**	o͞o	b**oo**t		circ**u**s
				ər	butt**er**

STRESS MARKS

Primary Stress '	*Secondary Stress* '
bi•ol•o•gy [bī **ŏl**′ə jē]	bi•o•log•i•cal [bī′ə **lŏj**′ĭ kəl]

A

ad•vice (əd vīs′) An idea for solving a problem: *Mary needed some good* **advice** *about how to keep her dog from jumping on the furniture.*

an•ces•tor (ăn′sĕs′tər) Family members who lived long ago. Great-grandparents and great-great-grandparents are our ancestors.

ANCESTOR

Ancestor comes from two words that mean "go" and "before." Ancestors are family members who have gone before you.

---

an•noy•ing (ə noi′ĭng) Bothersome; causing anger; not pleasing: *It is* **annoying** *if the phone keeps ringing while you are trying to work.*

anx•ious (ăngk′shəs) Eager to do something in a hurry: *Laura was* **anxious** *to get to the theater on time because they were showing her favorite movie.*

a•shamed (ə shāmd′) Feeling shame or guilt: *Marcy felt* **ashamed** *about returning the book two weeks late.*

at•ten•tion (ə tĕn′shən) Careful notice of someone or something: *If you pay* **attention** *to the directions, you will be able to make this model airplane.*

B

back•bone (băk′bōn′) The series of connected bones in the middle of the back; spine. The backbone is the main support of the fish's body.

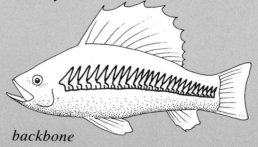

backbone

ă pat / ā pay / â care / ä father / ĕ pet / ē be / ĭ pit / ī pie / î fierce / ŏ pot / ō go / ô paw, for / oi oil / o͝o book /

breathe (brē*th*) To take air into the lungs and force it out: *We must breathe air to stay alive.*

C

ca•di•llos (kä dē yōz′) A prickly burr-weed that grows wild.

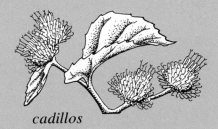
cadillos

com•mer•cial (kə mûr′shəl) An advertisement on radio or television that calls attention to a product: *I like watching the commercials for that new cereal with nuts in it.*

com•part•ment (kəm pärt′mənt) A separate section: *My backpack has two compartments: one for books and the other for gym clothes.*

con•sid•er•ate (kən sĭd′ər ĭt) Thoughtful of others and their feelings. If you are considerate of others, you try not to say or do anything that will upset them.

crea•ture (krē′chər) A living being; an animal: *Some creatures of the forest live in the highest treetops.*

cua•tro (kwä′trō) A musical instrument with a long neck attached to a sound box. It usually has four strings, which are plucked with the fingers or a pick.

cuatro

D

de•feat (dĭ fēt′) To beat someone in a contest: *Barbara always defeats Greg when they play checkers because she is a better player.*

oo b**oo**t / ou **ou**t / ŭ c**u**t / û f**u**r / *th* **the** / th **thin** / hw **which** / zh vi**s**ion /
ə **a**go, it**e**m, penc**i**l, at**o**m, circ**u**s

203

des•per•ate (dĕs′pər ĭt)
Almost without hope:
*Jennifer was **desperate**
because the game was
almost over and her team
still hadn't scored.*

dis•gust•ed (dĭs gŭs′tĭd)
Feeling sick and tired of
something; fed up: *Max
was **disgusted** with his
radio because he couldn't
fix it.*

dis•pleas•ure (dĭs plĕzh′ər)
A feeling of not being
pleased with someone or
something: *When I don't
clean my room, my
parents show their
displeasure by frowning.*

dread (drĕd) A strong feeling
of fear: *A feeling of **dread**
came over Sandra when
she entered the dark, scary
cave.*

en•chant (ĕn chănt′) Put
under a magical spell. If a
forest is enchanted, magic
things will happen there.

ex•pert (ĕk′spûrt′) A person
who knows or has skill in a
special area: *No one
thought the ship would
sink because the **experts**
had said it would not.*

ex•tinct (ĭk stĭngkt′) No
longer in existence. If a
group of animals is extinct,
none of that group of
animals is still alive.

fad (făd) Something very
popular for a short time:
*Wearing striped shoelaces
is a **fad** at my school.*

FAD

Fad is short for *fiddle-faddle*, an old
word that means "nonsense."

---

fault (fôlt) A bad habit, or a
weakness: *My worst **fault**
is that I can't wake up on
time in the morning.*

ă pat / ā **pay** / â care / ä father / ĕ pet / ē be / ĭ pit / ī pie / î fierce / ŏ pot / ō go / ô paw, for /
oi **oil** / o͝o book /

204

fes•ti•val (fĕs′tə vəl) A time when people celebrate together: *At the winter festival all the people in town get together to celebrate the first snow.*

festival

fos•sil (fŏs′əl) The remains of a plant or animal that lived long ago. Fossils are found in rocks and other substances that form the crust of the earth.

FOSSIL

Fossil first meant "something dug out of the earth" because most fossils were found there.

fossil

 G

gen•u•ine (jĕn′yōō ĭn) Not false; real: *I thought the coat was genuine leather, but the salesperson told me it was fake leather.*

gram (grăm) A unit of measure for weight in the metric system: *It takes 454 grams to make one pound.*

greed (grēd) A selfish desire for more than what one needs or deserves. When you take more than your share, you are showing greed.

grief (grēf) Great sadness over a loss; deep sorrow: *Pam was filled with grief when her cat disappeared.*

ōō boot / ou **out** / ŭ **cut** / û **fur** / *th* **the** / th **thin** / hw **which** / zh vision /
ə **ago**, item, pencil, atom, circus

hes•i•tate (hĕz′ĭ tāt′) To pause or hold back because of feeling unsure. A dog may hesitate to go near someone it does not know.

hor•ror (hôr′ər) Great fear: *The children screamed in* **horror** *during the movie.*

hu•mil•i•a•tion (hyoo mĭl′ē ā′shən) A feeling of deep shame: *Jim cried with* **humiliation** *when he fell down for the tenth time during the race.*

ig•nore (ĭg nôr′) To pay no attention to someone or something: *Randy turned away and tried to* **ignore** *Anna, hoping she would leave him alone.*

in•ter•view•ing (ĭn′tər vyoo ĭng) Asking a person questions to find out information: *Marsha* **interviewed** *her teacher for the school newspaper.*

in•ven•tion (ĭn vĕn′shən) Something made, created, or put together that did not exist before: *The new* **invention** *allows scientists to take pictures of the bottom of the ocean.*

leg•end (lĕj′ənd) A story that has been handed down from earlier times. It is not certain whether a legend is true or not: *I have heard many* **legends** *about the Wild West from my grandparents.*

mam•mal (măm′əl) One of a group of animals that have hair or fur on their bodies. Whales, humans, cats, dogs, cows, elephants, mice, and bats are all mammals.

ă pat / ā pay / â care / ä father / ĕ pet / ē be / ĭ pit / ī pie / î fierce / ŏ pot / ō go / ô paw, for / oi oil / oo book /

mis•chief (mĭs′chĭf)
Naughty or bad behavior:
My brother's **mischief**
always gets him into
trouble.

mum•ble (mŭm′bəl) To
speak unclearly: *When the*
teacher asked him a hard
question, he **mumbled** *the*
answer.

nerv•ous•ly (nûr′vəs lē)
Anxiously: *Martha waited*
nervously *to get on the*
plane.

nui•sance (noo′səns)
Someone or something that
is annoying; a pest: *Andy*
thought Linda was a
nuisance *because she was*
always asking questions.

numb (nŭm) Having no
feeling or unable to move:
Richard's toes were **numb**
from walking in the snow.

op•er•a•tor (ŏp′ə rā′tər) A
person who works a
machine or other
equipment: *The telephone*
operator *dialed the call for*
Mark.

out•wit (out wĭt′) To be
cleverer than someone else:
Glen **outwitted** *his brothers*
by finding out where they
had hidden the cookies.

Par•lia•ment (pär′lə mənt)
The government in
England.

Parliament

pa•vil•ion (pə vĭl′yən) An open structure with a roof, used for performances or shelter.

pavilion

pest (pĕst) A person who bothers other people: *Gary thought his cousin was a pest because he was always taking Gary's toys.*

pes•ter (pĕs′tər) To bother someone over and over again: *I wish you would stop pestering me with your questions when I am trying to read.*

pol•i•ti•cian (pŏl′ĭ tĭsh′ən) A person active in government. Mayors, governors, and presidents are politicians.

pop•u•lar (pŏp′yə lər) Enjoyed or liked by many people: *The book was so popular that the store soon ran out of copies.*

praise (prāz) To say that one admires or approves of someone or something: *Mr. Simpson always praises his students when they do a good job.*

res•cue (rĕs′kyōō) Save from danger or harm: *The firefighter used a ladder to rescue the cat from the fire.*

ro•bot (rō′bət) A machine that can perform human tasks and tasks a human cannot do.

ROBOT

In 1929 Karel Capek wrote a play about mechanical men who take over Earth and destroy all humans. He named these evil machines robots.

robot

ă pat / ā pay / â care / ä father / ĕ pet / ē be / ĭ pit / ī pie / î fierce / ŏ pot / ō go / ô paw, for / oi oil / ōō book /

S

sage (sāj) A very wise person.

scale (skāl) An instrument or tool used to weigh things: *I stepped onto the scale to see how much I weighed.*

scale (skāl) A small, thin part that forms the skin of fish and reptiles.

scale

sci•en•tif•ic (sī′ən tif′ĭk) Done by testing and observing in order to prove something: *Bonnie did a scientific experiment to see if tomato plants could grow without any light.*

seethe (sē*th*) To feel very angry: *The girl was seething when her brother broke her favorite toy.*

sig•nal (sĭg′nəl) To tell or make known with a sign, gesture, or device: *The ship used rockets to signal another ship nearby.*

sor•row (sŏr′ō) Sadness or grief: *Brian was filled with sorrow when he found out his cat was missing.*

sta•tion (stā′shən) A place with equipment to send out radio or television signals.

sur•vi•vor (sər vī′vər) Someone who has lived through an accident that caused the death of others: *There were about two hundred survivors in the airplane crash.*

sus•pi•cious (sə spĭsh′əs) Not trusting; doubting: *Carlos says he didn't hide my shoes, but I am suspicious because I saw him sneak in the back door.*

---

o͞o **boot** / ou **out** / ŭ **cut** / û **fur** / *th* **the** / th **thin** / hw **which** / zh **vision** /
ə **ago**, **item**, **pencil**, **atom**, **circus**

tease (tēz) To make fun of: *Kirk's brother **teased** him about the silly hat he had to wear for the school play.*

tem•per (tĕm'pər) An angry mood: *Robin says I have a bad **temper** because I am always frowning.*

vig•il (vĭj'əl) A period of time when someone is watching and waiting: *Hal kept **vigil** during the night, hoping his lost puppy would return.*

weight (wāt) The measure of how heavy something is.

weights (wāts) Objects on a scale that help measure how heavy something is.

weights

wor•thy (wûr'*th*ē) Of value; good: *The best woman was elected president because she was the most **worthy**.*

ă pat / ā pay / â care / ä father / ĕ pet / ē be / ĭ pit / ī pie / î fierce / ŏ pot / ō go / ô paw, for / oi oil / ͞oo book / ͞oo boot / ou out / ŭ cut / û fur / *th* the / th thin / hw which / zh vision / ə ago, item, pencil, atom, circus

210

Acknowledgments

For each of the selections listed below, grateful acknowledgment is made for permission to excerpt and/or reprint original or copyrighted material, as follows:

Major Selections

"The Hard-boiled Egg Fad," from *Ramona Quimby, Age 8*, by Beverly Cleary. Copyright © 1981 by Beverly Cleary. Reprinted by permission of Morrow Junior Books, a division of William Morrow & Co., Inc., and Hamish Hamilton Ltd.

"Henry Writes a Letter," from *Henry and the Clubhouse*, by Beverly Cleary. Copyright © 1962 by Beverly Cleary. Reprinted by permission of William Morrow & Co., Inc., and Hamish Hamilton Ltd.

The Loch Ness Monster, by Ellen Rabinowich. Copyright © 1979 by Ellen Rabinowich. Reprinted by permission of Franklin Watts, Inc.

"The Long-Lost Coelacanth," from *The Long-Lost Coelacanth and Other Living Fossils*, by Aliki. (Thomas Y. Crowell) Copyright © 1973 by Aliki Brandenberg. Reprinted by permission of Harper & Row, Publishers, Inc.

Mufaro's Beautiful Daughters, by John Steptoe. Copyright © 1987 by John Steptoe. Reprinted by permission of Lothrop, Lee and Shepard books, a division of William Morrow & Co. Inc. and the Estate of John Steptoe.

"Otis's Scientific Experiment," from *Otis Spofford*, by Beverly Cleary. Copyright © 1953 by Beverly Cleary. Reprinted by permission of Morrow Junior Books, a division of William Morrow & Co., Inc., and Hamish Hamilton Ltd.

The Rainbow-Colored Horse, by Pura Belpré. Copyright © 1978 by Pura Belpré. Reprinted by permission of Viking Penguin, Inc.

The Titanic *Lost...and Found*, by Judy Donnelly. Copyright © 1987 by Judy Donnelly Gross. Reprinted by permission of Random House, Inc.

"The Way People Live," from *Our Home the Earth*, by J. Oswald et al. Copyright © 1980 by Houghton Mifflin Company. Reprinted by permission of Houghton Mifflin Company.

Yeh-Shen, a Cinderella Story from China, by Ai-Ling Louie. Illustrated by Ed Young. Text copyright © 1982 by Ai-Ling Louie. Illustrations copyright © 1982 by Ed Young. Reprinted by permission of Philomel Books.

Poetry

"Look, Cinderella!" by Myra Cohn Livingston, from *A Song I Sang to You*. Copyright © 1984, 1969, 1967, 1965, 1959, 1958 by Myra Cohn Livingston. Reprinted by permission of Marian Reiner for the author.

"Sea Shell," by Amy Lowell, from *The Complete Poetical Works of Amy Lowell*. Copyright © 1955 by Houghton Mifflin Company. Copyright © 1983 renewed by Houghton Mifflin Company, Brinton P. Roberts, Esquire and G. D'Andelot Belin, Esquire. Reprinted by permission of Houghton Mifflin Company.

"Until I Saw the Sea," by Lilian Moore, from *I Feel The Same Way*. Copyright © 1967 by Lilian Moore. All rights reserved. Reprinted by permission of Marian Reiner for the author.

Quotations from Authors/Illustrators

Aliki (pg. 132), quotation from *Something About the Author*, Vol. 35. Copyright © 1984 by Gale Research, Inc. Reprinted by permission of the publisher.

Ai-Ling Louie (pg. 153), quotation from *Something About the Author*, Vol. 40. Copyright © 1985 by Gale Research, Inc. Reprinted by permission of the publisher.

Additional Acknowledgments

"Cinderella" (pg. 188), from the story by Ann-Marie Ekstrom. First appeared in Creative Kids Magazine copyright © 1987. Reprinted by permission of Creative Kids Magazine and the author.

"Letter from Beverly Cleary" (pg. 10), copyright © 1989 by Beverly Cleary. Used by permission of Morrow Junior Books, a division of William Morrow & Co., Inc.

Theme Books

The Theme Books shown on Extended Reading pages are available from Houghton Mifflin Company and are reprinted with permission from various publishers. Jacket artists for these books are listed below.

Beauty and the Beast, by Jan Brett. Jacket art by Jan Brett, copyright © 1989 by Jan Brett Studio, Inc.

Ramona Quimby, Age 8, by Beverly Cleary. Jacket art by Alan Tiegreen, copyright © 1981.

Sunken Treasure, by Gail Gibbons. Jacket art by Gail Gibbons, copyright © 1988 by Gail Gibbons.

Additional Recommended Reading

Houghton Mifflin Company wishes to thank the following publishers for permission to reproduce their book covers in Extended Reading lists:

Clarion Books, a division of Houghton Mifflin Company:
The Foundling, by Carol Carrick. Jacket art by Donald Carrick, copyright © 1977 by Donald Carrick.
Little, Brown and Company:
Cinderella, by Barbara Karlin. Jacket art by James Marshall, copyright © 1989 by James Marshall.
Karen Schmidt:
Aldo Applesauce, by Johanna Hurwitz. Jacket art by Karen Schmidt, copyright © 1979.
Scholastic/Madison Publishing, Inc.:
Exploring the Titanic, by Robert D. Ballard. Jacket art by Ken Marschall, copyright © 1988, by Madison Publishing Inc. First published in the U.S. by Scholastic Inc.

Credits

Program design   Carbone Smolan Associates

Cover design   Carbone Smolan Associates

Design   **8–71** Cross Associates;   **72–135** Pronk & Associates;   **136–191** Peter Good Graphic Design

Illustrations   **9–71** Renée Williams;   **73–75** Pamela R. Levy;   **76–77** Graham Bardell;   **76–78** Ken Marschall;   **80–83, 85** David Bathurst;   **86–87** Ken Marschall;   **89** David Bathurst;   **92–93** (map) Jack McMaster;   **94** Jack McMaster;   **96–98** Ken Marschall;   **100–108** Aliki Brandenberg;   **109** Graham Bardell;   **116, 118** Kathleen Volp;   **119** David Rose;   **121** Jack McMaster;   **122** Gustave Doré;   **123** David Rose;   **124** (diagrams) Jack McMaster;   **126** Kathleen Volp;   **128** (top) David Rose;   **129, 130** Jack McMaster;   **131** Ian Carr;   **132–133** Rene Milot;   **135** Graham Bardell;   **137–139** Lynne Cherry;   **140–153** Ed Young;   **154–169** Connie Connally;   **170** (top) Reprinted by permission from The Random House Book of Fairy Tales, © 1985; (bottom) By permission of Houghton Mifflin Company, © 1989;   **171** (top right) Published 1971 by Dover Publications, Inc.; (bottom) By permission of Neugebaur Press, Salzburg, Austria, © 1988;

172–185 John Steptoe;   **187–191** Lynne Cherry;   **194** (map) Precision Graphics;   **202, 203** (top left) Robin Brickman;   **203** (right) Sharron Holm/Cornell & McCarthy;   **205** (left) Sharron Holm/Cornell & McCarthy;   **207** Susan Banta;   **208** (right) Sharron Holm/Cornell & McCarthy;   **209** Susan Banta

Photography   **11** Courtesy of Beverly Cleary;   **76** Illustrated London News Picture Library;   **77** (right) Dave Gray/Woods Hole Oceanographic Institution;   **78** (right) Ken Marschall Collection;   **79** (top and center) Harland and Wolff/Ken Marschall Collection; (bottom) Ken Marschall Collection;   **84** (left and center) Ken Marschall Collection; (right) Illustrated London News Picture Library;   **90** Ken Marschall Collection;   **91** Daily Sketch;   **93** Dave Gray/Woods Hole Oceanographic Institution;   **95** (top) George F. Mobley/National Geographic Society; (bottom) Woods Hole Oceanographic Institution;   **99** Tom Kleindinst/Woods Hole Oceanographic Institution;   **110–111** (all) Jeff Rotman;   **112–113** The Production Company/The Image Bank;   **114–115** UPI/Bettmann Newsphotos;   **117** AP/Wide World Photos;   **120** Marty Snyderman;   **121** UPI/Bettmann Newsphotos;   **125** Kindra Clinef;   **127** Scottish Daily Record & Sunday Mail;   **128, 130** AP/Wide World Photos;   **132** (left) Courtesy of Judy Donnelly; (right) Courtesy of Aliki Brandenberg;   **133** Rich Cook;   **153** Adrian Kologi;   **169** Courtesy of *Something About the Author*;   **186** Courtesy of Ann Armistead White;   **193** (center, top left, and bottom right) David G. Houser; (bottom left) Dr. R.L. Jackson;   **195** David G. Houser;   **196** Jacques Jangoux/Peter Arnold, Inc.;   **197** Victor Englebert;   **198** (all) Owen Franken/Stock Boston;   **205** (right) Dennis M. Dennis/Tom Stack & Associates, Inc.;   **208** (left) Eunice Harris/The Picture Cube;   **210** Richard Megna/Fundamental Photography;   **Back cover** Courtesy of Ann Armistead White

End Matter   production by Publicom, Inc.

212